Hardly a Jockey

Hardly a Jockey

John Hislop

MARLBOROUGH/PUNCHESTOWN

MARLBOROUGH BOOKS
18B Ash, Kembrey Park, Swindon, SN2 6UN

c/o 9 Queen Street, Melbourne 3000, Victoria, Australia

PUNCHESTOWN BOOKS
4 Arran Quay, Dublin 7

First published 1993

Typesetting and Origination Footnote Graphics, Warminster.

Jacket Design *Ron Stephens*.

ISBN 1–873919–12–3 Marlborough
ISBN 1–873920–07–5 Punchestown

Printed and bound in Great Britain by
Biddles Ltd, Guildford and King's Lynn

CONTENTS

1

REVERSION TO TYPE

The war was over. As a regular officer once expressed it, "now we can get back to proper soldiering." But soldiering no longer concerned me; having been demobilised, I had put the Army behind me for ever. In 1945 I had married my wife, Jean, a widow whose first husband, Captain R.E.M. Thackeray, had been killed in the invasion of France in 1944. My mother, who died in 1941, had left me enough money to produce a modest income, sufficient to enable me to view finding a job desirable rather than essential. Before the war my aim had been eventually to become a flat race trainer; now this no longer appealed to me. The profession was not as I used to know it and I had neither the temperament nor desire to adapt myself to the changes. Besides, having lost five years of race-riding I wanted to make up for it while I was still young enough, and this would not have fitted in with training racehorses.

Shortly after the war Fred Darling, one of the greatest trainers of the century, who was then in poor health, asked me to go to him as an assistant and then take over the stable when he retired in a couple of years' time; but even this did not tempt me to change my mind. I have never regretted the decision. My old boss, Victor Gilpin, the trainer whom I joined at Newmarket in the Clarehaven stable as a learner, joined the Army at the outbreak of war and retired when he was demobilised, first to Ireland and then to Berkshire, dying in 1975 at the age of 85. My time with him is recounted at length in *Far From a Gentleman*.

The closest link with my pre-war racing life was Tom Masson, for whom I had ridden before and during the war and who trained at Lewes. Tom Masson was an outstanding horseman and horsemaster, whom I got to know through Victor Gilpin when I was with the latter at Newmarket. Then farming near Welwyn Garden City, Tom also dealt in hunters, rode show jumpers, schooled horses and had been a successful point-to-point rider. He was a tall, well built man with strong, even features, was good company and had great success with women. Tom used to ride show jumpers and hunters for the circus owner Bertram Mills; in fact he once performed in a circus act, which entailed galloping into the ring and jumping some obstacles, as if out hunting. Once, the horse he was riding missed his stride, hit the jump and turned a somersault, at which the audience applauded amid laughter, believing it was all part of the act. Luckily horse and rider were none the worse. Through his association with Mills' Circus, Tom learnt a number of tricks of the trade known to few horsemasters, which helped him greatly in dealing with problem horses for which he was famous when he became a trainer of racehorses, a number of which found their way into his yard from other trainers unable to cope with them, and were reformed by Tom. Among these was Pindari, sent to Tom from Harry Wraggs' stable because he was given to rearing and walking about on his hind legs, whom Tom put right and sent out to win the Lingfield Derby Trial Stakes. Pindari was one of the horses brought down in the Derby of 1962, won by Larkspur.

Before the war I used to go over to Tom's farm on non-working days, when the racehorses were only walking, to improve my riding, and spent a winter with him. This was invaluable experience and taught me a great deal about horsemanship, which not many have the chance of learning. Later Tom gave up farming and set up as a trainer at Lewes, when I rode for him often, mostly over fences and hurdles, before and after the war. In Tom's name I rented a small farm at Chailey, near Lewes, called Simmonds Farm, which Tom occupied and ran during the war. The house consisted of two rooms upstairs and two downstairs, the bathroom being on the ground floor, off the kitchen. By the end of the war, Tom had moved back to his yard, Barn Stables, at Lewes, on the opposite side of the road to the prison, and my wife Jean and I occupied Simmonds Farm. Thus, while many looked back on the war years as the happiest of their life and were trying to readjust themselves to former jobs or learn new trades, I slipped smoothly and imperceptibly back into the world so familiar to me and in which I have always been at home, that of the Turf. I was then thirty-four, an age at which a steeplechase rider's career is approaching its end, if it has not already been reached. But I was determined to ride over fences again, even if only for a season or two and to continue for several more on the flat. Apart from an injury which put me out of action for eighteen months, the outcome of a fall in a steeplechase at Cheltenham, I had kept pretty fit during the war, nor was I troubled by weight. So it was little problem to get back into race-riding condition. For an amateur rider, the importance of fitness cannot be overestimated. There is all the difference between exercise riding and race-riding; and a moderate amateur who is really fit will beat a good one who is not. To have had a thorough grounding of fitness, involving regular race-riding over a period of years, is a great help to regaining the necessary condition after a long interval. I believe that the run of success which came my way on the flat immediately after the war was due largely to my having devoted so much attention to keeping fit while the war was on. As a result, I had the edge on those of my riding contemporaries who, either through no fault of their own or from choice, disregarded this aspect. None of my younger opponents of that time were lucky enough to have had my background of riding work regularly and on the racecourse before the war.

It is not always easy to gather up the threads of a race-riding career if they have been dropped for any length of time. This applies especially to jumping when a rider has been out of action through injury, since there are only too many ready to believe or impute that he has lost his nerve. Sometimes he has, but whether true or false it does not make the climb back any easier. Much depends upon luck. A few early winning rides can dispel the suspicions of doubters, and instead of 'he's on the amber' or 'he's seen the red light', the rider's reappearance is greeted in terms of 'the break has done him good'. Courage is a strange quality, governed largely by circumstances and mental outlook. It is determined neither by youth or age, pugnacity or physique; it is often present where least expected and absent when it might be taken for granted. Possibly the key to courage is enthusiasm for the aim, when thoughts of attainment alone fill the mind and there is no room for speculation on the consequences. At only one period during my riding career have I ever felt a complete lack of nervousness before a race. This was during the war, perhaps through contrast with the more undesirable alternatives which war offered as compared with the racecourse.

It was with curiosity, therefore, that I awaited my reactions to riding over fences again. I was soon to find that the days of nonchalance had gone for ever. Where once, for a short time, I rode without a care, now my tactics were tempered with fear of possible injury, which often causes accidents through indecision. With the uncertainty of life during the war, hazards of the racecourse offered nothing to lose; indeed, they might be the means of a welcome alternative to tedium, or death. With the return of peace, the whole outlook changed. Life had much to offer, there was time to be made up in activities and projects shelved during the past five years, and those who emerged from the war unscathed had no desire to receive in peacetime damage which military service had failed to inflict, not necessarily in battle, since a high proportion of wartime casualties have nothing to do with the enemy. It was so with me. I wanted the best of both worlds: to enjoy the thrill of riding, without the risk of injury. So I determined to pick my rides over fences with care, which, as all who understand the game know, marks the beginning of the end of a steeplechasing career. To turn down suicidal rides is one thing, to pick and choose indicates the sowing of the seeds of hesitation, which sooner or later grow into faulty judgment and lack of initiative.

My first post-war ride over fences was in 1945, on a horse named Milk Bar. He was a tall, handsome grey gelding, hard to fault except that he had a little too much daylight under him, then eight years old, by Miracle out of Take a Glass, by Tetratema.

During the war I had bought a half-share in Milk Bar with Tom Masson, who acquired him on the advice of George Lambton; and when N.H. racing ceased in England we sent him over to Ireland to be trained by Tim Hyde, who won the Grand National on Workman and used to ride that brilliant Cheltenham Gold Cup winner, Prince Regent. Milk Bar had run second for us on the flat at Windsor, and in Ireland won a 'chase and a hurdle race, being disqualified after winning again over hurdles. When I married I bought Tom's share in Milk Bar and gave him to Jean as a wedding present. He did well, winning a number of 'chases, despite going wrong in his wind and having to be tubed. His greatest attribute was his jumping, which was bold, fast and safe. He had a fine turn of speed, no doubt due to the influence of his maternal grandsire, Tetratema, who was by The Tetrarch and was a brilliant horse up to a mile, winning The Two Thousand Guineas and twelve other races.

Milk Bar did not stay more than two miles over fences and hurdles but was especially effective downhill, having beautifully sloped shoulders, excellent forelegs and a smooth, powerful action. As a result he was eminently suited to Plumpton, where he won several times. There the technique was to drop him in behind for the first circuit, slip through on the inside at the fence on top of the hill last time round and let him go down the slope for all he was worth. He gained lengths at each downhill fence and so great was his reach that any horse trying to take him on at a fence was in danger of being jumped down. This manoeuvre gave him a lead which usually he was able to hold to the winning post.

My first ride of all on Milk Bar was in a hurdle race at Fontwell on November 3rd 1945. He ran promisingly to finish third to Port o'London, a useful and extremely good-looking horse by Blue Peter and, respectively, trained and ridden by Fulke Walwyn and Frenchie Nicholson. In second place came a consistent mare called Sun Cheer, ridden by John Cox, who later, for a number of years, was our stud groom.

Milk Bar next ran third, again over hurdles, to two good horses, The Diver, owned by Jakie Astor (Sir John Astor), and Vidi. Then, rather surprisingly, he fell over hurdles at Fontwell. His downfall came as a result of over-confidence: he stood too far back and his forelegs went between the top two bars as he was coming down, but we emerged unhurt; and, as every jumping jockey knows, a soft fall is good for morale. We then decided to run Milk Bar over fences.

The schooling fences at Lewes had not been rebuilt, so we ran him without his having seen a fence since he returned from Ireland. However, he jumped them boldly and in good style in Ireland, and as the obstacles at Windsor, where he was to run, were not stiff, the venture could hardly have been termed hazardous. All the same, I was apprehensive and realised only too clearly that the euphoria of the war years had vanished. As it turned out, my forebodings were groundless: Milk Bar jumped fluently, finishing third to two useful handicappers, Astrometer, ridden by Dan Moore, a fine Irish rider, for Miss Dorothy Paget, and Sidmouth, formerly a good 'chaser and winner of his previous race. Milk Bar won his next two races, both at Plumpton, gave me a good ride in the Cathcart Challenge Cup at the National Hunt Meeting at Cheltenham and ended the year by running second at Cheltenham and third at Fontwell where, because I had 'flu, he was ridden by Dick Black, who later in his career won on him at Cheltenham when I was recovering from 'flu.

The most dramatic race in which Milk Bar and I were involved was the following season, on his favourite battleground, Plumpton. It was the Ovingdean Handicap 'Chase, run over two miles, and worth £137 to the winner, but it was the medium of a huge gamble on the part of one of the biggest bettors of that era, Major W.H. Mackenzie.

Mackenzie, who was I believe a Canadian, owned one or two horses under both Rules and on this occasion backed a 'chaser of his called Domino to win a fortune.

Domino was a good-looking bay gelding, who showed considerably more quality than the average 'chaser. He was by Noble Star, at that time about the only notable tail male descendant of St. Simon standing at stud in England and winner of the Jockey Club Cup, Ascot Stakes, Cesarewitch and Goodwood Stakes. Domino was a half-brother to Tiffin Bell, who bred the Cesarewitch winner, Chantrey, and was trained at Weyhill by Frank Hartigan. Frank's son, Joe, a good rider who later trained at Middleham in Yorkshire, finished third on Domino in the National Hunt 'Chase at Cheltenham, but the horse never lived up to his looks. On this occasion Domino opened at 10/1 in the betting and was forced by a tidal wave of money down to 3/1. We had backed Milk Bar, perhaps rashly in the circumstances, but the money was placed before the furore for Domino developed. My own investment was £100. Milk Bar was a popular horse at Plumpton, where he was always well supported, because of his liking for the course and being trained locally; after coming into the betting at 6/1 he finished second-favourite at fives. Domino, who was ridden by Bob Turnell and carried 10st. 7lbs, received 16lbs from Milk Bar. At this advantage his stable appeared to have considered Domino unbeatable.

Milk Bar was so accustomed to the tactics which we adopted at Plumpton that he could have carried them out on his own. We lobbed along smoothly and effortlessly behind the leaders for the first circuit, slipping through on the inside to lead into the fence at the top of the hill, after passing the stands for the second time. Then I sent him along as fast as he could go. At each fence he took off outside the wings, landing as far on the other side, and at the bottom of the hill he was clear of his nearest opponent, which was Domino, though from my position I was unaware of it. As the ground levelled out and deprived Milk Bar of his topographical advantage, Domino began to close the gap and Bob Turnell adroitly manoeuvred him through on the inside after landing over the station fence to challenge going into the last. Domino's presence and the sight of the fence in front of him made Milk Bar renew his efforts and I rode him into it with hands and heels. In the fourteen races in which we competed together I never drew a whip on him. Bob was driving Domino for all he was worth and as we neared the obstacle we were really travelling. Two or three strides away I could see that we were meeting the fence wrong; either Milk Bar was going to get too close to it, or take off so far back that he would seem bound to hit it. Domino, who was galloping dead level with him, was similarly placed, but being more compactly built and having a shorter stride he was better equipped to put in a short one. As we neared the fence I sat up straight, anticipating the worst and left the rest to Milk Bar. He picked up a terrifying distance from the fence and, I suppose instinctively, because the two horses were racing stride for stride, Domino did the same. The force of Milk Bar's take off, added to my sitting up straight, fearing disaster, resulted in my being 'left behind', and I gave him the full length of the reins to counter-act this lapse of equitation. But he never touched a twig, landing yards away on the far side. Not so Domino. He simply did not possess the reach and power to enable him to emulate Milk Bar's stupendous leap, crashing through the top of the fence and shooting Bob up in the air. They rejoined each other on landing and Domino kept his feet, but the impact slowed him up. Meanwhile, Milk Bar had gained a clear lead.

This decided the issue. Though Domino rallied and ran on gallantly he had no hope of making up the lost ground. I had only to keep Milk Bar going with my hands to have three-parts of a length to spare at the finish. Milk Bar won the race again the following season, carrying 12st. 1lb. and starting at 6/5. The opposition was weak and we won comfort-ably, but this was his last victory. By then he was beginning to lose his dash and was high in the handicap. So we gave him to Joe Hartigan, who wanted an inexpensive horse to ride himself, ensuring him a good home. He gave Joe one or two safe but unsuccessful rides and then developed navicular disease and was put down. Milk Bar was something of a character and not the easiest of horses to ride at exercise. He was lively and had a disconcerting habit of shaking himself violently, wrench-ing his rider's knees away from the saddle, and then bucking. As often as not this resulted in the rider finishing on the ground, which Milk Bar appeared to find entertaining, as he then stood still until remounted. Milk Bar was cured of this habit by my riding him one day with a surcingle which had a short broom-handle attached to it, so that the handle came across my knees and stopped me from falling off. When he bucked and received two or three strokes of the whip from my left hand, finding he could not dislodge me, he gave up the attempt and never tried it again. Milk Bar was 'done' by Harry Hannon, a slightly built Irishman then working for Tom Masson. After leaving Tom, Harry Hannon set up training on his own with some success. He gave me several rides, including one on a hurdler called Henri Quatre, who carried me courageously to a narrow victory in the last race of the Boxing Day meeting at Kempton in 1947, being the only favourite to win in the two days. Henri Quatre's owner was known in the racing world as Manure Monty, his business being fertilisers.

Harry Hannon's son Richard, now master of the large and prosperous East Everleigh stable in Wiltshire, has little of his father about him in build or accent: he has the frame of a rugby football forward and his speech smacks of Berkshire rather than Ireland. A cheery, pleasant character, who never lets the vicissitudes of the game get him down, Richard Hannon knows the business thoroughly, among his innumerable winners being The Two Thousand Guineas winners, Mon Fils, Don't Forget Me and Tirol.

During the same period, I partnered a most attractive horse over hurdles, called Prince Paramount. He was a brown, virtually black, entire horse by Suzerain (by Son-in-Law) out of Porphyr, by Rose Prince, of beautiful quality, a little over 16 hands, strongly and squarely built with a smallish, intelligent head and excellent limbs. Tom Masson and I bought him out of the late Harold Wallington senior's stable for Jack Dennis, a friend of pre-war days in Sussex, who had ridden as an amateur over fences when in the Life Guards and owned a horse or two. Prince Paramount had won on the flat during the war, a mile-and-a-half maiden race at Pontefract, trained by Cecil Ray, a South African who rode with success on the flat in England shortly before the war and then took out a trainer's licence. Prince Paramount moved to Harold Wallington after Ray lost his licence as a result of one of his horses having been found to be doped. I fell in love with the horse as soon as I set eyes on him, Tom liked him too and we bought him, so far as I remember, for £1,000.

At that time, the 1944–45 jumping season, Tom's jockey was Matt Feakes, a good rider who later trained many winners including King's Bench, successful in the Coventry Stakes, the Middle Park Stakes, and the St. James's Palace Stakes, and second to Thunderhead II in The Two Thousand Guineas. Naturally, Matt rode Prince Paramount in his three races that season. The horse proved a fine jumper and finished second first time out, at Cheltenham. Next he ran at Windsor, where he was third and in his final outing of the season, at Cheltenham, he was unplaced in a good class field, but ran well.

The following N.H. season Matt was not retained by Tom, and Jack Dennis, for whom I had ridden occasionally before the war, asked me to ride Prince Paramount. No prospect could have pleased me more. I have always been a horse snob, having a penchant for high-quality, good-looking individuals, as opposed to those of plebeian appearance; and Prince Paramount was just my type.

We first appeared together at Fontwell, where he ran third. Since it

14

was his initial race of the season and he was some way short of his best, the performance was satisfactory. His next race was again at Fontwell, where he was opposed by a good horse called Firoze Din, who had finished third to Owen Tudor and Morogoro in The Derby of 1941, when trained by George Todd. Firoze Din had changed ownership and stables and, now a 7-year-old gelding, had developed into a first class hurdler under the care of Fulke Walwyn, later becoming a good 'chaser. Having won his previous two hurdle races with great ease, Firoze Din was a hot favourite. He was a tremendously hard puller, but went well for Sean Magee, a stylish and effective jockey who had learnt his trade in the academy of the Dr. Arnold of the Turf, Stanley Wootton. Firoze Din won easily, but Prince Paramount was beaten only three lengths, which showed that he had improved markedly since his previous race.

Prince Paramount's first success was at Southwell on November 17th, 1945. It was not a race of any consequence, a maiden hurdle worth £100 to the winner, and he only won by a neck; but the circumstances were significant with regard to his next race, because a loose horse interfered with Prince Paramount going into the last hurdle, causing him to lose impetus and enabling the horse racing with him, Tavistock, a half brother by Tai Yang to The Oaks winner Pennycomequick (by Hurry On), to gain a couple of lengths. This incident passed without comment in the accounts of the race, so that on the face of it the form did not look good.

On November 30th we took Prince Paramount to Cheltenham for the second division of the Haresfield Novices Hurdle, a race of far higher status than the one at Southwell. Hot favourite at 8/11 was Salver, a handsome, compact, if rather flashy, chestnut horse by King Salmon out of Versicle. On the flat he had been trained by Jack Colling, and had the misfortune when a three-year-old to run up against the subsequent Derby winner Ocean Swell and, next time out, to encounter Tehran, who won that year's St. Leger, Salver finishing second each time.

Though Salver won a good maiden race at Newmarket later, he must have found these previous two encounters chastening experiences. Before meeting Prince Paramount at Cheltenham, Salver had run second to Carnival Boy, a top-class novice hurdler, who was destined to finish second in the Champion Hurdle. It was not surprising, therefore, that Salver was made a strong favourite. Despite this, our stable took him on with hope verging on confidence, supporting the view with hard cash. The decision was based, firstly, on Salver having given the impression of being not entirely resolute; secondly, on the assumption that he was not a true stayer which, added to his dubious courage, was not a good omen for so exacting a course as Cheltenham with its gruelling, uphill run from the last hurdle to the winning post; thirdly Prince Paramount was an out-and-out stayer who would battle to the end and was much better than his last form suggested. We all had a good bet on him, Jack Dennis adding to his commitment by laying Salver. Prince Paramount ended up at 100/8.

Traditionally Cheltenham is not a front-runner's course, because its contours and run-on are so severe; but it was decided that I should go on with Prince Paramount, in order to make the utmost of his stamina and probe that of Salver to its depth. Fred Rimell was riding Salver, who was trained by his father Tom. Prince Paramount was a delightful ride, his only fault being that he could not quicken; this was probably the reason why he ran disappointingly when ridden by Matt Feakes, who used to wait with him.

Prince Paramount was amenable to making the running, which the rest of the field appeared only too willing to let him do. He galloped along in this position, jumping perfectly and enjoying himself as much as I was; then Salver drew up to him between the last two hurdles on a tight rein. Though tall for a jockey, Fred Rimell was as stylish as he was strong and competent – before becoming too heavy he rode 34 winners on the flat – and even on a small, compact horse such as Salver, who had rather a short neck, he tucked himself away as neatly as any flat race jockey and more so than most. Fred used to go into his fences or hurdles with a short hold of the horse's head, but always gave him plenty of rein to land, if he needed it. As we went into the last hurdle Salver took a slight lead; from the stands he must have looked home and dry. In my mind I can still see the two horses in mid-air, as if in a photographic 'still'. Perhaps it was the dramatic quality of the instant, emphasised by the money I stood to win, that imprinted this picture so vividly and indelibly on my memory. But Salver's lead as he landed did not worry me; I was convinced that he would not last out the uphill run-in from the final hurdle and, indeed, this proved so. Hand ridden, Prince Paramount regained the lead, going on to win by a length.

Not long after this, Tom Masson and Jack Dennis fell out and Prince Paramount left to be trained by Peter Cazalet. He continued to win, first over hurdles and later over fences, ridden by the stable jockeys. I have written at some length about Milk Bar and Prince Paramount because they were the two horses to bridge the gap between my former and postwar riding life. They gave me the confidence I needed at this period and I owe them much.

16

The following season I was lucky enough to get the ride on the best hurdler of his day, National Spirit, in an amateurs' race at Fontwell. In the course of his career, National Spirit won the Champion Hurdle twice and may have been unlucky not to win it a third time, when he did not get the best of runs. This misfortune was counterbalanced by luck being on his side in 1947 when his rider, Danny Morgan, a top-class jockey and a particularly stylish and strong finisher, who made use of his knowledge of the intricacies of Cheltenham to go the shortest way, whereas Alec Head, a leading French jockey who afterwards attained even greater distinction as a trainer, rider of the second, Le Paillon, did not know that route. Since Le Paillon won the Prix de l'Arc de Triomphe the same year there seems little doubt as to which was the better horse of the two.

When I rode National Spirit he was emerging from the novice stage, having won twice after finishing second and being three times unplaced, all at minor meetings. He was owned by Len Abelson, a businessman who had two or three horses in training, some with George Todd, National Spirit being with Vic Smyth at Epsom. Vic Smyth was one of a family famous on the Turf, being a brother of Nat (Herbert) and an uncle of Ron and Ted, the former a champion N.H. jockey and a successful trainer. Vic Smyth was a top-class flat race jockey in the 1920s, an era of great riders, who finished second in The Oaks on Soubriquet, and third in The Two Thousand Guineas and Derby on, respectively, Captain Cuttle and Hurstwood. By the time I knew him, Vic was training, at which he was proficient and successful, his victories including The One Thousand Guineas with Zabara. He liked a punt, was a good judge of racing, but believed in making it fun. Like his brother, Nat, he was always cheerful and witty and I greatly enjoyed his company on the race-course. I rode for Vic again some years later, when Teddy Underdown, a friend from pre-war days who was a stylish amateur on the flat and did quite well as an actor, could not do the weight on a sweet little French-bred entire horse called Pont Cordonnier in a bumper race at Lewes. Pont Cordonnier was completely different to National Spirit, being sensitive, refined and light-mouthed. He gave me a beautiful ride, winning by a short head, after a long battle in which I never drew my whip.

Having begun his racing career unimpressively and being on the upgrade, National Spirit had been underestimated by the handicapper and was given only 10st. 12lbs. Meyrick Good, for many years the senior racing correspondent on *The Sporting Life*, had engaged me to ride a horse for him in the race, but when he saw how National Spirit was handicapped he thought it was not worth opposing him, so released me

17

for National Spirit, whom Vic Smyth had asked me to ride soon after I had accepted Meyrick Good's offer.

National Spirit was a big, powerful, lengthy chestnut gelding with a prominent white blaze, by The St. Leger winner Scottish Union out of Cocktail, by Coronach, who won The Derby and St. Leger. There was more of Coronach than of Scottish Union about him, and like the former he took a pretty strong hold. He had markedly flat withers, as a result of which the saddle was liable to work forward; this occurred with Gordon Richards on one occasion at Lingfield, when it finished virtually up his neck, but National Spirit still won.

The day did not start propitiously. We had a flat tyre on the way and got to the course only just in time for me to weigh out. In fact Dick Black, then an amateur, was standing by ready to take the ride in case I failed to arrive soon enough. There were six runners, none of whom had been placed last time out, so that National Spirit's price of 13/8 on was remarkably generous. All he had to do was get round without my falling off. My instructions from Vic Smyth were to hold him up until we had turned for home. In view of the quality of his opponents and National Spirit's strength, keenness and superior ability, this brief represented a task verging on the herculean. However, Vic Smyth, like George Todd, for whom I was to ride a great deal during the next few years, expected jockeys to carry out their orders, if they hoped to ride for him again, and I determined to anchor National Spirit whatever happened. I succeeded and he won easily by three lengths, but I was unable to straighten out my arms for some time afterwards. His jumping was sketchy at times, probably due to the slow pace and my having to restrain him most of the way.

National Spirit went on to win innumerable races, both on the flat and over hurdles. In amateur races on the flat he was ridden by Teddy Underdown, who rode out regularly for Vic Smyth and was put up by him in bumper races. National Spirit never won a bumper race nor did he run again with an amateur up over hurdles. After a long and honourable career he was retired and lived to an old age, having a race at Fontwell named after him.

2

RIDING FOR GEORGE TODD

One of the first flat-race meetings I attended after the war was Salisbury, which with the return of peace had reverted to the pre-war system of only letting members into the chief enclosure. The result was chaos and, in a less orderly country, would have ended in a riot. Many pre-war members had died, either from old age or as a result of the war, a number had let their membership lapse, and few, if any, new members had been made. In consequence, there were only a handful of people in the members' enclosure, but a large, furious crowd, packed like sardines in Tattersalls, most of whom wanted to get into the members and, as a result of accumulated pay and allowances from military service, war contracts, black market deals or the sale of articles acquired under the heading of the spoils of war, were well able to afford the entrance fee. The few of us who had kept up or renewed our memberships found ourselves in spacious comfort.

It was a two-day meeting and on the opening day George Todd, a trainer for whom I had ridden once or twice, asked me if I would ride a horse trained by him, called Gremlin, in the bumper race on the following day. I jumped at the opportunity, as it was the first amateur flat race to take place after the war and I was particularly keen to get a ride in it. A few minutes later Eric Stedall, a trainer I had known for some years, asked me to ride a horse for him, which I had to turn down. Eric was an agreeable, gentlemanly character, who trained for pleasure rather than profit and mostly for friends. He had a deceptively prim manner, and when learning to train with Jack Leader at Newmarket, was persuaded to attend a dinner party dressed as a clergyman. The company was somewhat taken aback when 'his reverence's' anecdotes became more

19

and more bawdy as the evening progressed before his true identity was revealed. By an odd coincidence Eric Stedall and George Todd, during the war, shared the yard at West Ilsley where Dick Hern trained later. In 1945 George bought Manton, moving in for the 1947 season and spending the rest of his life there. George Todd died in 1974.

A coincidence in the story of Gremlin was that he had started his racing career in Eric Stedall's stable and was bought by George Todd at the end of his three-year-old season, when still a maiden, for Desmond Baring, a former cavalry officer and amateur rider whom, with his wife Mollie, Jean and I had known from pre-war days. Gremlin was a beautifully balanced, good-looking bay gelding by Felstead out of Merry Life, by Sir Cosmo. He was a delightful ride and had a fine turn of speed, but could only sustain his finishing run for about two furlongs. "You'll do your boots betting on this one", Harry Wragg remarked to George Todd after being beaten on Gremlin at Hurst Park; but, through waiting on him, Wragg had come with too long a finishing run, which Gremlin could not maintain. George emphasised Gremlin's peculiarity to me and I was careful to carry out his instructions. The outcome was that Gremlin won easily by three lengths from Royal Glory, ridden by Frank Cundell, and Carnival Boy, a top-class hurdler, ridden by Ronnie Strutt (now Lord Belper). Eric Stedall's horse, Prince Cosmo, whom Ginger Dennistoun rode, was fourth.

While the result was satisfactory, the style of my performance left much to be desired, as I let Gremlin run home on a long rein, without picking him up, and must have looked like a tripper riding a donkey on the sands. Charlie Smirke, who had won the New Greenham Stakes the previous day on Fine Lad, the substitute race being run at Salisbury instead of Newbury, its usual home, was the first to point this out to me. Charlie, with whom I had ridden work in my pre-war Clarehaven days, was always a great help to me with riding advice. A superb jockey himself, he could also discourse on the intricacies of the art with clarity, explaining the cause and nature of errors, whether of style or tactics, and how they could be corrected. All my racing life I have had cause to be grateful to professional jockeys, both on the flat and under N.H. rules, for gratuitous help and instruction. If Charlie Smirke had not had so much trouble with his weight, he might well have rivalled even Gordon Richards for champion jockey. I never encountered any ill-feeling on account of my being an amateur; it is not amateurism itself that the professional dislikes, it is incompetence.

I have two unhappy memories of Gremlin, both involving hurdle races. One was at Wolverhampton, where I thought he was sure to win and had a fair bet on him. In fact, as he landed over the last just behind the only danger left in the running, Your Fancy ridden by Dick Black, I felt certain we would win, as Gremlin had such a good turn of finishing speed. He was on the inside where a few yards after the last hurdle there was a false rail to protect the ground for flat racing. At the end of the railed-off strip was a single rail across the protected ground. Just after he landed, Your Fancy came across Gremlin, so that he had nowhere to go except straight at the rail which sealed off the protected strip. He crashed through this, thereby putting himself out of the course, so that technically he ran out. Thus, though he actually finished second, he was no longer in the race. Gremlin's owner, Desmond Baring, lodged an objection to the winner, but it was automatically overruled because Gremlin had finished outside the course. Even if Your Fancy had been disqualified it would have been no help since the third horse, Querneuville, not Gremlin, would have got the race. The experience shook Gremlin's confidence badly and he never showed his best form after it, though running fifth in the Liverpool Hurdle. Some years later a sequel to this race occurred. It was at one of H.M. Prisons, I think Wormwood Scrubs, an institution in which, happily, I found myself as a member of a quiz-team and not as an inmate, though the decor and environment recalled memories of my boarding school days. During the session, members of the audience posed various questions to the team, which the one most conversant with the subject of the question endeavoured to answer. One of these questions was: "Would Mr Hislop tell us what happened to him on Gremlin at Wolverhampton?"

While the incident at Wolverhampton was pure bad luck, the other, which occurred in the Imperial Cup at Sandown, was entirely my fault. There had been a great deal of rain preceding the race, though it was fine on the day, and as a result there was a patch of ground just after the entry to the straight, towards the rails, which was a morass. I walked the course beforehand and made a note of where the bad ground lay, but on turning into the straight, lying second or third, I miscalculated the position of the morass, thinking it was closer to the rails than it was, and ran straight into it. I realised my fate when Frenchie Nicholson on the winner, Tant Pis, who was just in front of me, swung wider, but it was too late for me to follow him, since by then we were right on top of the bad patch. As a result Gremlin was stopped almost to a walk and all hope of winning vanished. I was mortified. The Imperial Cup then carried the prestige which later the Schweppes Hurdle acquired and I longed to ride the winner of it as much as Desmond would have liked to have won the race, which his father-in-law, Ben Warner, had done in pre-war days with that grand horse Residue. Whether Gremlin would have won or not it is impossible to say, but he was going extremely well at the time and I would have been surprised if he hadn't gone close to victory.

What Milk Bar and Prince Paramount were to me over fences and hurdles, Gremlin was to me on the flat: he set me on the path to success which carried through the ten remaining years of my riding life, though I only lasted a short spell over hurdles, a shorter one still over fences.

While Gremlin was the horse who brought about the start of this good fortune, it was his trainer, George Todd, who was largely responsible for enabling me to maintain the run. I had ridden once or twice for George Todd before the war, over hurdles, though not a winner. The nearest I got to it was being beaten a neck on Priddy Hill by Staff Ingham on Durex in a long-distance hurdle race at Gatwick. It was not George's fault that I did not ride a winner for him before the war. He offered me the ride on Priddy Hill in an amateurs' hurdle race at Newbury, but unfortunately I had already agreed to ride another, Cottage Owl, trained by Geoffrey Pease. Priddy Hill won comfortably under the expert guidance of Harry Applin, while Cottage Owl was unplaced. When I realised that George Todd was prepared to put me up regularly, I never engaged myself for a race in which George had an entry without consulting him first.

Many years ago someone remarked to George Lambton "Why don't you bring *'Men and Horses I have known'* up to date?" Since this is the best book of Turf reminiscences ever written, the question was not surprising. However, the answer came: "The horses are there, but where are the characters?" In an age greatly changed since the days of *'Men and Horses'*, it is understandable that George Lambton should have found no characters to intrigue him; yet in my time there have always been personalities who by their individuality, eccentricity, strength of character, virtues or faults, stand out from among their contemporaries. One of these was George Todd. A tall, lean, slightly formidable figure, always well turned out in a style which could be termed neat, not gaudy, George attained a position in racing of admiration and respect. This was gained by ability, determination, initiative, hard work and courage. He was not born into the racing world and had to make his way up from the bottom. Coming from Lincolnshire farming stock, he was put to work on the land as a boy; but the plodding tempo of rural life was too turgid for his nature which, despite a somewhat puritan background, had in it a touch of the gambler. He was ambitious and prepared to take a chance, which agriculture could not offer. So he turned his back on the mud of the Lincolnshire fields and set out on the springy footing of the Turf, finding employment with the Newmarket trainer Bert Lynes. A stable lad's life in those days was hard. Wages were meagre, days were long and the week's work comprised its full seven days; except in cases of sickness or death, days and weekends off were unheard of and annual holidays, when they could be afforded, were brief. A bicycle was the only form of transport. Beer, betting and 'baccy' were the chief solaces outside working hours. Horses had to be groomed meticulously and vigorously, so much so that more than a few thin-skinned ones were turned bad-tempered, if not savage, by this; stables, boxes and tack had to be cleaned to perfection. Head lads sometimes exerted a discipline compared with which pre-war sergeant-majors would have seemed like probation officers. An old-timer told me of an occasion when one hit an apprentice on the head with a feed-bowl, because he was not quick enough in opening a box door when going round with the head lad during the early morning feed, killing him; somehow the affair was hushed up and no action was taken. Over all was the spectre of the sack, which in any profession in the 1920s was a disaster. Yet few old-timers I have known regretted their life; if they had not possessed the necessary skill, resilience, will to work, and dedication to the profession they would not have lasted in it.

George Todd was one who stood up to this spartan regime and reaped the reward of survival and intelligent absorption of all that was to be learnt from it. He was always too tall and heavy to have any hope of becoming a jockey, so determined that he would eventually be a trainer instead. His diligence and skill as a stable worker took him up the scale quicker than most and he became head lad first to Bob Colling and then Tom Coulthwaite.

If I had to choose a trainer between an ex-head lad and an ex-jockey I would go for the former every time. Races are won and lost primarily in the stable, by good or bad feeding, as the case may be. This does not mean just cramming as much corn into a horse as he will eat, which will sooner or later produce undesirable repercussions, but studying him as an individual and feeding him accordingly. "You should feed a horse up to his work, not work him up to his feed", George used to say. This art can only be acquired from experience resulting from feeding many different horses, allied to intelligent observation and flair, which a head lad has the best possible opportunity of acquiring.

In the area of the stable the successful jockey has limited experience. As an apprentice he will have learnt to 'do his two', but little or nothing about feeding or the care of legs, let alone have had the experience of hundreds of different horses, which a head lad has enjoyed. As regards working horses, a jockey seldom sees them other than on galloping mornings, nor does he have experience of the long, dreary but essential weeks of winter and early spring exercise, which lays the foundation of a successful season. "An Ascot Gold Cup horse's preparation starts at Christmas," George Lambton opined. Instead, the jockey is likely to be savouring warmer climates or riding on the all-weather tracks. Ex-jockeys, therefore, have to rely largely on their head lads for guidance in the stable and on the training grounds, except for galloping mornings. This is not to say that an intelligent, hard working ex-jockey cannot learn from observation and experience: "When I started to train I hardly knew which end the corn went in", a former jockey, who later became a highly successful trainer, once remarked. The chief problem with the ex-head lad is the office work, race planning and finding owners, with which the ex-jockey is better equipped to cope. The average modern owner has no idea whether a horse is being badly or well trained and feels it smarter to have his horses in the care of someone who is a household name than with a trainer of whom none of his friends are likely to have heard, however competent he may be. Thus the head lad who takes the plunge into the deep waters of training has a tough struggle ahead of him, unless fortunate enough to have a rich patron behind him.

George certainly dived in at the deep end. When he began training, in 1925, he had little money and about three horses, renting modest accommodation at Royston. He used to work his horses on some ground which Captain Percy Whitaker, a former amateur rider of note and for a time Master of the Oakley Hunt, used for his jumpers. Percy used to ride a good 'chaser called Silvo, of whom Munnings painted a portrait, with Percy in the saddle. Silvo was owned by Mr. W. H. Midwood, a fine supporter of jumping. I got to know Percy quite well when I was working at Newmarket and, in fact, rode a winner for him over fences at Huntingdon shortly before the war. He was squarely built, of medium height, military appearance and pleasant company, but liable to be choleric in the early morning. "Where the hell's Rory O'More?" – a well-known 'chaser trained by Whitaker – he bellowed at his head lad one morning. "I told you to get him out first lot and he's not in the string", embellishing the remarks with some powerful and vivid adjectival clauses. When, at last, he drew breath the head lad was able to inform him, "You're on him, Sir". At one time Percy Whitaker had a mixed stable of over forty horses, among them Silvo, Arravale and Mount Etna, all successful 'chasers; this was at St. Giles near Salisbury in the 1920s, which must have been before he moved to Royston and, later, to Newmarket. When I knew Percy he only had two or three horses, among them Knight Error, with whom he won the Lincolnshire Handicap in 1931, and an attractive mare called Anna (by Hurstwood), who was a good handicapper and won the Newbury Cup. He also trained the Royal Hunt Cup winner of 1935, Priok, a plain, angular, light-framed French-bred gelding by Asterus. Neither Percy Whitaker nor his successor at Royston, Roy Pope, would let George use the flat race gallops at Royston, so he moved to East Ilsley and finally to Manton, now owned by Robert Sangster, and occupied by his son-in-in-law, as the resident trainer, Peter Chapple-Hyam. The arrangement could not have worked out better, as the young trainer moved straight into the top rank with victories in The Derby (Dr. Devious), Two Thousand Guineas and Champion Stakes (Rodrigo de Triano) and other notable winners.

Robert Sangster himself, outside the Arabs, is probably the most powerful and successful owner-breeder in the world. Born on May 23rd 1936, he is of medium height and athletically built, quiet and unobtrusive in manner, punctilious in business dealings, fearless of opposition on the racecourse and a bold bettor. Famous winners to carry his 'emerald green, royal blue sleeves, white cap, green spots' are too numerous to list, suffice it to say that he has won The Derby with The Minstrel and Golden Fleece – he was unlucky to lose it narrowly with El Gran Senor, who won The Two Thousand, and bred the 1992 Derby winner Dr. Devious.

Apart from his victories on the racecourse, Robert Sangster is in the happy position of owning, partly or wholly a bunch of unusually good stallions, among them Sadlers Wells, Caerleon and Lomond. He is a member of the Jockey Club.

From the time I first rode Gremlin, I got to know George Todd well. When we moved to East Woodhay House near Newbury, in 1949, I used to go over to Manton regularly to ride work, usually twice a week. It was a pleasant drive in the stillness of the early morning, through Kintbury and along the road that leads over a succession of bridges, past the water meadows and on to the Bath road; through Marlborough's spacious, still sleeping main street, narrowing as it passes through the College, John

Betjeman's alma mater and that of Ian Balding and John Dunlop, where I once attended a field day when at Wellington, and finally turning right off the Bath road and up the hill to the Manton stable.

For me, one of the charms of the Turf has been its associations: its history, traditions, characters, human and equine, its dramas and its tragedies. As a boy and young man I had read every book on the subject I could find, even the tedious and ponderous three volumes of Sir Theodore Cook's 'History of the Turf'; and accounts of famous racing stables, their occupants and the men concerned with them never failed to fire my imagination. One of the most important training stables was Manton. I never knew Alec Taylor, the most famous of the trainers at Manton, though he was just within my time; but his successor, Joe Lawson, who had been Taylor's head lad, I knew. Among the great horses trained at Manton in the past I had read of such as Bayardo, Gay Crusader, Picaroon, Book Law, Saucy Sue and Buchan, so that to be associated with the stable in the shape of 'first bumper' to George Todd was to become part of a great tradition, minor though this part might be. George never had more than some thirty horses in his stable, because he could not otherwise give them the personal attention he deemed necessary. He did all the feeding himself and knew every horse inside out. Owners he regarded as necessary evils only to be tolerated if he had virtually complete control of the horses, many of which he owned himself, entirely or partially. Financially, George started from nothing. He built up his fortune by betting, which enabled him to buy Manton, and but for being an inveterate punter, often losing a great deal of money on other people's horses, he would have been considerably richer. His training career did not start auspiciously. The first runner he fancied and on which he had a good bet was beaten. He was puzzled, as he thought it was sure to win and could not understand why it did not. It was the last race of the day and he remembered that he had left his macintosh in the weighing room, so went back for it. As he was collecting it, he overheard the jockey who had ridden his horse and the rider of the winner laughing and recounting how the former had stopped George's horse and both had gone for the winner. George told the owner, who I think was Horace Lester the bookmaker, for whom I rode a number of winners trained by George, saying, "Don't worry, we'll get our money back". The next time the horse ran he was ridden by one of George's apprentices, was ignored in the market and won. This experience had a lasting effect on George, as it made him suspicious of jockeys other than his own apprentices or lads, with the result that he

26

lost a number of races through putting them up in place of experienced jockeys.

By the same token he often put up amateurs instead of professionals over hurdles, on the principle that he knew where he was with them, though he once told me that he ceased using an eminent pre-war amateur because he found him a bit too hot.

Though George lost some races through employing apprentices, and I lost him one I should have won, he had some good touches using apprentices or 'bumpers'. Of one such coup I only heard after his death, though it occurred during the period of which I write. George had a beautiful chestnut horse called Gala Performance, by Stardust out of Extravagance, by Bahram. He was strong, squarely built, but full of quality and was not raced until he was three. He had a run in a good maiden race at Newbury and later appeared in one of lesser calibre at Salisbury. George put up on him one of his apprentices, who had never before ridden in a race; not unnaturally Gala Performance was '25/1 others' in the betting among twenty-five runners. George and Horace Lester, who owned Gala Performance, backed him away from the course and he won by four lengths. Not a soul on the course knew that the stable had had a penny on, including one of George's other owners who was staying with him, nor George's wife, Audrey, till he said to her in the kitchen when clearing away the plates between courses, "I had it off today, but don't you bloody well look pleased when you go back into the dining room." Gala Performance next ran in The Derby; he was out of his element and made no show, but went on to win a good many races during his career.

I greatly enjoyed going over to ride work at Manton and talking to George Todd. We used to walk up to the gallops, taking the two dogs, an Airedale, Stormer, and a cairn terrier, Rusty. George liked to walk for the sake of the dogs and because he could have a close look at the gallops, about which he was meticulously particular. He would tell me about his early days with Tom Coulthwaite, who started as a trainer of runners and had never been on a horse in his life, but became the leading trainer of jumpers of his day and sent out the Grand National winners Eremon, Jenkinstown and Grakle. Coulthwaite was a hard trainer and his horses had to stand up to a stupendous amount of work, but seldom were let off the bit; "draw upsides over the last two furlongs and finish roonin away", were his usual instructions to his work riders.

Coulthwaite was a keen rose-grower and Harry Brown, the last amateur to head the list of N.H. riders including professionals, who often

27

rode for him told me that Coulthwaite always asked a lad he was interviewing for a job whether he liked gardening, before any other query. Coulthwaite would never let anyone mix the feeds but himself, and when he went away he left each feed made up, with a rose-label bearing the horse's name attached to it. Harry Brown told me that Coulthwaite boasted that he never had to tell a jockey to stop a horse if he didn't fancy him: he stopped him in the stable by fixing his feed.

In those pre-war days dope-testing was almost non-existent and most trainers had their own pet tonics, most of which would never get through the net today. Fred Darling used Fowler's solution of arsenic, which was then considered a tonic rather than a dope, but since it contained strychnine it would not be allowed now. Fowler's solution was a two-edged sword, being liable to cause sterility and, indeed, some of the fillies trained by Darling had poor records at stud. Darling raced his top horses sparingly and usually retired them as three-year-olds, doubtless to avoid reaction from an accumulation of arsenic in the horses' system, as this substance does not pass out of the body. George Todd told me that on one occasion Coulthwaite, before he left for a meeting, gave him strict instructions to feed a certain horse as usual only with the feeds he had left for him, and about his work. The horse, Windermere Laddie, a good hurdler, was engaged in an important race in a few days' time and was to be ridden in the race by Staff Ingham, who was also to ride him work. He was to do two canters, then seven furlongs sharp and finally a steady two miles over hurdles, finishing in the customary manner 'roonin away'. George was to take particular note of how the horse went and report to Coulthwaite in detail. The instructions were carried out to the letter and the horse went appallingly; on his performance he would not have won anything. "But it didn't put me off," George said. "Tom Coulthwaite knew that Staff and I both liked a bet and I was sure that he had fixed the horses with something in his feed before leaving so that, as a result of his working badly, we would not back him and thus not spoil the market. I had a good bet on him and he won."

With only some thirty horses in his stable, George was able to give full, personal attention to each, and work-mornings took place in a relaxed atmosphere. There was none of the mad rush to get through in time, which occurs in big stables, when batches of horses come by like grouse with the wind behind them and it is no mean feat to discern and memorise how each went, let alone have a good look at them when they have pulled up. I have known of a batch coming up when the trainer has

28

started for home, having forgotten all about them. Though George virtually never had his horses off the bit, he trained them thoroughly, but with imagination, varying the distances over which he worked them, at the same time giving them plenty of experience over the full extent of the horse's race. They had at least half an hour's walking before they worked and were usually out about two hours in all. Stayers or gross horses often had an hour's walk in the afternoon as well.

His method of working was to set off in single file, drawing upsides going into the last two furlongs and finishing 'roonin away'. The horses were always good rides, because they had been taught to settle and were not stirred up. As a result of these methods George's horses, when they came to race, always ran right out to the bitter end. If they were beaten it was because they had come up against a better horse on the day. I never remember riding a horse trained by George that tired under me, and they sometimes were involved in close finishes. The patient and pains-taking treatment he gave to horses enabled him to rehabilitate those who had been soured or had lost their confidence, and since for many years he was only able to buy inexpensive horses, those of this category were liable to find their way into his stable, often repaying him hand-somely for his consideration and skill. Another feature of his training was that he was able to make horses stay further than their breeding suggested, because he taught them to run relaxed until picked up for their final effort, and because they were sent out really fit. In appearance George's horses were distinctive: they always looked bright and healthy in their coats, the skin loose, were thoroughly muscled, but not light, and had a certain leanness about their necks, which from the days of Alec Taylor seemed to have been a trademark of the Manton stable. I think it resulted from the nature of the ground over which they walked and worked, the time they spent out at exercise and the amount of work they did over the full distances over which they usually raced. This was more marked in the days of the Taylors, who were severe trainers, than of George Todd.

As may be imagined from these observations, George was a grand-master in the art of training stayers. During the decade under review he won the Chester Cup with Retsel, by the Derby winner Pont l'Eveque; the Goodwood Stakes twice with French Design, who also won the Cesarewitch and was by Coup de Lyon and, like Gremlin, out of a mare by the sprinter Sir Cosmo; and the Queen's Prize with Gremlin and Romney Legend. In later years he trained Sodium to win The St. Leger and The Irish Sweeps Derby, and Oncidium, successful in the Coronation

Cup and Jockey Club Cup. One of his most remarkable feats was to win the Goodwood Stakes with French Design the year after he won the Cesarewitch, without an intervening race. Few trainers would be capable of this. I have no clear recollection of his Chester Cup winner, Retsel, except that he was a bay, not unlike his sire, Pont l'Eveque. His name was that of the surname of his owner, Horace Lester, spelt backwards. I rode a number of winners for Horace Lester, who I believe was George's first patron. He was a bookmaker from the Midlands, a dignified elderly gentleman, with a white moustache and a quiet manner more in keeping with a churchwarden than the popular conception of a bookmaker, and an admirable owner, uncomplaining in defeat, modest in victory. A good supporter of the Turf for many years, Horace Lester was consistently successful without having expensive horses. The H.S. Lester Memorial Challenge Cup at Salisbury perpetuates his name.

Among the horses I rode for Horace Lester and of whom I have fond memories was Fair Oration, a light-framed, narrow, bay gelding by Fairford. He had the courage of a lion, was a beautiful ride and an effortless, free mover with quite a nice turn of speed. Technically he was no more than a good plater; but in his class he was hard to beat and he carried me to victory on several occasions, notably in the Carnarvon Cup at Salisbury three years running. The 1953 running of this race produced a measure of drama. Fair Oration was favourite at evens, second favourite being a horse trained by Fulke Walwyn called Loreley, who was ridden by Teddy Underdown and belonged to Mrs Jack Thursby, who died in an air accident some years later. Nothing else was seriously fancied. In a desperate finish Fair Oration and Loreley dead-heated and in so doing Loreley came over on to Fair Oration, squeezing him against the rails. In those days the lodging of objections was a somewhat delicate matter: the stewards seldom objected off their own bat and some owners never lodged an objection, on principle. As I returned to the weighing room, Jimmy Park of the *Evening Standard*, one of the ablest racing journalists of his day, remarked, "People may not think it's the thing to do to object in an amateur race, but you're sure to get it if you do." I answered, "I'll leave it to the owner." When I returned to the winners' enclosure and dismounted George and Horace Lester were there to meet me. George said, "We must object, we're certain to get the race." As I entered the weighing room, John Alexander, a retired naval officer of some seniority and a delightful character, said to me: "Are you going to object?" I said "Yes, the owner wants to; we're sure to get it." "Don't say that," he said, and disappeared. It transpired that he was an acting steward, which I had not appreciated, and that the stewards were going to lodge an objection on their own account, if I was not.

Outside there was quite a stir. Objections in amateur races were simply not the thing. Added to this Teddy was a personal friend, so the whole affair was fraught with social niceties. So far as I was concerned, it made no difference whether I objected or not; a dead-heat counted as a winner and I had not backed the horse, as I did not think that the price represented value for money. But George and Horace Lester were differently placed; each had had £1,000 on Fair Oration, so the financial difference between winning and dead-heating was appreciable. No one seemed to have given a thought to the public, many of whom would have been involved since, owing to my run of luck in amateur races in this decade, many punters backed my horses blind and put them into multiple bets. In retrospect, I should have objected myself, provided the owner agreed, in the interest of the public, but in the climate of the day this never occurred to me. The late Robert Morley, the actor and a keen racing man who did well as an owner on a small scale, and was a friend of Jean and myself, ran into another mutual friend, the late Michael Dawson, and in support of the thespian profession, Teddy also being on the stage, expressed the view that it was sure to be overruled. "I'll bet you a tenner it won't," replied Michael, and the bet was struck. "The easiest tenner I've ever collected," Michael observed after the objection was sustained. Though deserving to be given the race, Fair Oration might have been a lucky winner, since next time out Loreley won a higher class handicap at Birmingham by four lengths; if he had kept a straight course and not come across on to Fair Oration, I think Loreley would have won outright as he was running on and Fair Oration had no more to give.

Apart from riding all George's runners in 'bumper' races on the flat, I rode a horse or two for him over hurdles before giving up riding jumping. One of these was a mare belonging to Horace Lester called Miss Blighty, by Rameses the Second, sire of the Cheltenham Gold Cup winner Red Rower. Rameses the Second stood at East Woodhay House Stud, which we bought in 1949, but by then there was no stallion standing there. The race in question was a selling hurdle at Windsor, for which Miss Blighty was a firm favourite at 2/1. When George went to saddle Miss Blighty he found that she was in season, so decided to halve the stable commission. He had arranged to back the mare for one of his owners, Sir William Cooke, an old gentleman who was very deaf. He beckoned Sir William into the parade ring in order to get this information through to him. Accompanied by Lady Cooke he joined the group comprising George, myself and the travelling lad Wally Mills. George was having an uphill task trying to tell Sir William that he was reducing his bet from £200 to £100, because the mare had just come into season. The old man kept nodding his head, saying, "That's right, £200," when Lady Cooke came to George's rescue by shouting in her husband's ear, "You stick the lot, it doesn't make any difference the first half hour." She was right; Miss Blighty won comfortably by two lengths.

I rode a number of winners for the late Sir William Cooke in his purple, scarlet sleeves and cap; these colours, along with those of several other eminent owners of the era, decorated the cardboard cover of the annual Badminton diary of the era. Small, thin and neatly built, Sir William had been a first-class polo player as a young man, but had been forced to give up the game for medical reasons. Despite his condition he possessed boundless energy, hunted a pack of hounds, took them to every meet, rode home with them and saw them done up for the night. Another of his accomplishments was that he was an expert coaching whip. He was also a knowledgeable and successful orchid grower. When I knew Sir William, which was from 1945 till his death in 1964, he had left his native Yorkshire and owned Wyld Court, near Newbury, where he lived and had his stud. He was an indefatigable racegoer and keen punter. In his day he owned three notable horses: Hornet's Beauty, Dark Legend and Happy Knight. Hornet's Beauty, who was foaled in 1908, was a bay gelding by Tredennis out of Hornet, by Hackler. Before he appeared on a racecourse he was being hawked around Ireland for £100 with no takers. Steve Donoghue, who must have known something about the horse or discerned merit in him, advised Sir William to buy him; but it was not until Hornet's Beauty had won three races that he did so and then had to pay £2,000 for him. Hornet's Beauty proved a goldmine, winning 31 races and at one Royal Ascot meeting the Trial Stakes, Fern Hill Stakes and King's Stand Stakes. On another occasion Hornet's Beauty was the centre of a demonstration at Newmarket. He was entered for the Cambridgeshire and had been well backed for the race by the public, but was struck out and started for another race at the meeting, which he won, the horse and his owner being given a hostile reception on returning to the winners' enclosure. It was said that this episode was the cause of Sir William never being elected to the Jockey Club.

On one of Sir William's horses I had a sharp lesson and was lucky to get away with it. The horse was a chestnut colt, called Papist, by

Tom Masson on his hack at Lewes in 1947.

Milk Bar (J.H.) at the last fence before upsetting a gamble on Domino (Bob Turnell) at Plumpton.

Kami (J.H.) at the start.

Gremlin (J.H.) and his owner Desmond Baring after winning at Kempton. This combination, with trainer George Todd, won 4 times on the flat and a hurdle race.

Precipitation out of Valuable, by Canon Law. The scene was Windsor, August 18th, 1949. As all who know this course will appreciate, the finishing line is deceptive: horses which appear to have won by at least a neck are sometimes found to have been beaten. In those days there was no photo-finish camera, but it would not have made any difference. Papist had the race won comfortably and, with a view to his handicapping in the future, there seemed no need to win further than was necessary, so I allowed him what seemed to me a clear half-length. When I heard the verdict given as a short-head, I could hardly believe my ears. In fact the winning distance was probably a bit more, since the judge remarked to me afterwards, with a smile, "I thought I'd give you a bit of a fright, so I made it a short-head." I never took a liberty at Windsor again.

Sir William Cooke retained his enthusiasm and energy to the last; he died in his 92nd year after a few days' illness. I always found him courteous, modest, a good judge of racing and of horses and a man who raced for the fun of it. Though he liked a bet it was the excitement rather than the money that intrigued him. Always neatly dressed, he invariably wore a bowler hat, but seldom an overcoat, however cold the weather. He was one of the old school, who might have come out of George Lambton's delightful book 'Men and Horses I have Known', set in the Edwardian era. Towards the end of his life he sold Wyld Court, retaining only the orchid houses, which have been kept going successfully by his daughter Betty. I went over to Wyld Court before the sale, to look at the tack that was coming up, and ran into Sir William who talked to me about the coaching days when his father was alive, telling me how before the invention of horse-clippers the carriage horses were lathered and shaved, instead of being clipped.

Another of George's owners for whom I rode several winners was Darcy Halford, a wine merchant. A suave, tallish, rather distinguished looking man, with an engaging character and a good sense of humour, Darcy also had a horse or two elsewhere, including the Manchester November Handicap winner of 1949, Fidonia, trained by Snowy Parker at Epsom. Darcy was knowledgeable about racing and a shrewd, careful punter; he was not a heavy bettor, but usually collected when he put his money down and was prepared to back his opinion. Once at Ascot I was riding a horse for him called Technique, a half-brother by Casanova to Papist. He was an attractive, beautifully balanced little chestnut colt and a pleasant easy ride who had carried me to victory at Windsor in Darcy's 'white, sky blue sleeves, yellow cap' and at an earlier meeting at Ascot, each race being at a mile-and-a-half.

Technique was a genuine horse, but for some reason George sometimes ran him in blinkers, which he wore when he won his previous race at Ascot. This time the race was two miles. When I came to weigh out there were no blinkers and George said: "I must have been thinking of something else, I forgot to declare the blinkers." –In fact I was pleased that he had omitted to do so, because I thought that the two miles was as far as he liked to go and that the blinkers might make him run too freely and, in consequence, that he might not get the trip. I told George and Darcy this before the race, but I think George must have been a bit doubtful of my theory, as the horse was fairly easy to back at 9/4, starting joint favourite with Lode, a big, fine-looking brown gelding owned and ridden by Jakie Astor, who had won a number of races on him, trained by Jack Colling.

George usually got several people to do his betting for him, each going to a different bookmaker. His commission agents as a rule were Bill Carter, Snowy Chalmers and Joe Aldmark, though at times he varied the system by putting someone else in, or placed his bets away from the course. George always had a bet on his horses if he thought they had a chance at all, since whenever he did he included a bit for 'the yard', the proceeds going into a pool shared by the lads in cash at Christmas. He might say to me before I got up on one of his horses, "I've had £100 on him for the yard, in case he comes up, but I don't think he's good enough to win."

On this occasion George may have taken such a view because, while Darcy was standing near the rails a bookmaker beckoned him over and said, "The Todd mob haven't backed your horse, I don't think he can be fancied." "Really," said Darcy, "What'll you lay me about him?" "You can have 5/1 if you like," was the reply. "I'll take it to a couple of hundred," said Darcy and strolled off to watch the race, leaving the bookmaker to ponder the wisdom of the transaction. Sometimes everything goes right for a jockey in a race, at others everything goes wrong. For me this was one of the days when luck was on my side. I had a lovely smooth run all the way round on the rails and was able to slip through on the inside coming round the last bend, taking second place to Jakie on Lode, who was going extremely well. In those days Ascot had not been rebuilt, nor the course altered, the run-in being some eighty yards longer than it is today. Thus the tactical position was entirely different to what it is now; and as we turned for home the thought immediately came to me, "at all costs I must not hit the front too soon." If I did so, Lode, who was a true stayer, would almost certainly run Technique out of it. So I pulled

38

in behind Lode and stayed there until going into the last furlong, when I eased him out and picked him up for his final effort. Technique answered gallantly, getting up to win by a head. As the course is today, it would have been risky to have waited so long. I doubt if any race gave Darcy more pleasure.

An owner of George Todd, for whom I rode a good deal, was Percy Thompson, the bookmaker. Then a young man, he was one of the boldest layers on the rails and himself a fearless gambler: once he bancoed the late Aga Khan at the big table at Deauville – and lost. A warm, good-natured character, Percy was plump, fresh-faced and energetic. He owned a number of horses with various trainers, mostly with George Todd, and his colours 'purple, mauve star back and front' were familiar to racegoers then. At that time it was possible to buy French horses worth the money, and most of Percy's horses were acquired in France. I think one of his other trainers, John Goldsmith, who had been brought up in France and had a distinguished war record with the Special Services there, found them for him. John trained a top-class 'chaser for Percy called Le Jacobin.

The two horses I rode for Percy, which I remember best, were French: Coubrador and Philadelphe II. Both were fine individuals, Coubrador an out-and-out stayer, Philadelphe II a middle-distance horse. Coubrador, who ran second to Strathspey in the Cesarewitch, carried me to victory in an amateurs' race at Ascot and in the Coronation Hurdle at Liverpool.

It was by accident that I came to ride Coubrador over hurdles. Jean and I had been for a holiday in the South of France, which nearly ended in divorce through the inactivity of Cote d'Azur life, causing me to observe, as we sat in the sun on the Promenade des Anglais, at great expense, "What wouldn't I give to be riding out with George Todd at Manton!" Immediately after our return we went to Sandown. I had no ride, in fact I had not been on a horse for some three weeks, and was standing on the steps of the weighing room before the first race when George Todd came up to me and said, "Will you ride Coubrador in the next?" The jockey he had engaged, I think it was Tim Molony, had not arrived and he was forced to find a substitute at the last moment. I explained that my condition was not the acme of fitness, but that if he was prepared to put up with this I would be delighted to ride. George said, "That's quite all right, he's got no chance, but I want to give him a run." The race was the Otley Hurdle; there were only four runners, but one of them was the best hurdler in training, National Spirit, ridden by Bryan Marshall, so the result was a foregone conclusion. Having no thought of riding, I had not warned my valet, Charlie Stalker, to bring my tack. He had no difficulty in fitting me out, but when I got up I found that after pulling my leathers up as far as they would go I was still riding some three or four holes longer than my usual length. Fortunately Coubrador did not pull, so it did not matter, though when I cantered down to the post I felt as if I was out hunting rather than on the racecourse. Coubrador gave me a pleasant ride to finish third, National Spirit winning easily from a French-bred horse, of whom I have no recollection whatever.

Coubrador's next engagement was the Coronation Hurdle on March 23rd, 1949, the opening race of the Aintree Grand National Meeting, and to my delight George asked me if I would like to ride the horse there. The race carried considerable prestige and took a good deal of winning. There were fifteen runners, the only one ridden by an amateur being Coubrador, who started joint favourite with Cresta Cup, a horse owned by the late Duke of Norfolk, trained by Ivor Anthony and ridden by Martin Molony, a brilliant rider both on the flat and under N.H. Rules. From the start the race was run at a furious pace and Coubrador, who took time to warm up, was one of the last pair rounding the paddock turn; the other was Cresta Cup. As we were making the bend Martin called across to me "We're all right here, they'll never keep this pace up." He was right. Gradually the field came back to us and Coubrador was able to take the lead approaching the last hurdle to win comfortably by two lengths from Bow and Arrow; Cresta Cup, who in this class did not stay, finished third.

I rode Coubrador twice more, in a three-mile hurdle race at Kempton and at Cheltenham. At Kempton he made a bad mistake at the hurdle in front of the stands, fell on his head and shot me over it. The form book solicitously recorded the mishap as 'fell', but I don't think that Coubrador actually turned over. This completely destroyed his confidence, for at Cheltenham he went with no zest at all, tailing himself off, and I pulled him up. He never ran over hurdles again.

Philadelphe II had quite a different temperament to Coubrador. He was keen, taking a strong hold, and when he arrived at Manton was nervous and impetuous. This was due to the way he had been ridden in France, where he was jumped off and sent along from start to finish, receiving plenty of stick in the process. George at once started to restore his confidence. He fitted him with a cross noseband, sometimes termed a Grakle noseband, because the Grand National winner of that name used to wear one; and in all his work Philadelphe II was kept in behind other horses, so that he learned to settle. Formerly he had reached a stage when, as soon as the whips started going towards the end of a race, he would drop right out, hoping to avoid further punishment. He did win the Rosebery Stakes, making all the running, but this was not the way George wanted him ridden and these tactics were the outcome of Cliff Richards not obeying orders, or Philadelphe II taking charge of him. Luckily no horse got near him, or he would have dropped out of the battle. I used to ride Philadelphe II often in his work and got to know him well. In amateur races he was virtually unbeatable, as he carried weight without difficulty and when held up could produce a devastating turn of foot at the finish. His best distance was a mile-and-a-quarter, but he won up to a mile-and-a-half. I rode Philadelphe II many times and was only once beaten on him, in a race at Birmingham, a first-class racecourse but set in depressing surroundings which, added to the local populace not being race-minded, kept casual racegoers away. Professionally, Birmingham is a great loss; the going was always good, it had a long run-in, the draw made no difference, it was flat and the bends were nicely graduated. Philadelphe II being keen and a hard puller, I always started him in the heels of the other runners – there were no starting stalls then – to make certain of getting him covered up, and before I went out George always used to remind me to make sure that I did so. This day, for some reason, he did not emphasise this, saying instead, "I shouldn't leave him too much to do; lay handy all the way." So instead of starting just behind the others, I lined up level with them, intending to pull him in behind the leaders after jumping off. As it happened, Philadelphe II left the gate fast, nothing else went with him and I could not get him covered up. From that moment all chance of winning had gone. I tried to persuade him that he was having it all his own way, sat still on him when the others drew level, in the hope that he would realise that he was not going to be hit, and spoke to him persuasively; but these artifices had no effect, he just quietly dropped out of the battle. It was the one time I let George down and I could have wept.

Another of George's owners, whose horses I sometimes rode, was Sidney Banks, a farmer and corn merchant of standing who lived near Sandy in Bedfordshire. A keen hunting man and later a Master of Hounds, Sidney bred and raced horses, sometimes training jumpers at home, as his son does now. Of the horses I rode for Sidney Banks, two I remember particularly: Goodnight, a sweet little bay gelding, neat and light-actioned, who won on the flat with me; and Stipend, a hurdler, also a bay gelding, well made and stronger than Goodnight, but not having as much quality. Goodnight was of especial interest to me, since Victor Gilpin used to train his dam, Counterpane, an attractive little mare by Manna out of Lamb Mint and owned by the Duke of Norfolk. Counterpane was a small winner and came from a distinguished family, her grandam Scotch Gift having bred Tetratema; unfortunately the family did not return to this status. Stipend was the means of upsetting a gamble in an amateurs' hurdle race at Windsor on a horse called Welsh Pet, owned and trained by Jack Reardon. Though Stipend was favourite at 7/4 and Welsh Pet started at 6/1, this did not mean that Jack Reardon had not backed Welsh Pet. He knew that in Stipend, a useful and consistent hurdler who would be well supported, he had strong opposition in the betting and by going in at the right time he would get a good price. In addition Welsh Pet was receiving 8lbs plus a 5lb riding allowance which David Punshon, a pupil of Jack's and later a successful professional, was able to claim, so that Stipend was giving 13lbs in all. Punshon had been well schooled by Jack, who from a small stable produced Harry Sprague, the best hurdle race rider of his day and a good jockey on the flat until increasing weight forced him to concentrate on hurdle racing, Jock Wilson and Brian Swift, both successful flat race jockeys; so that Punshon's 5lb riding allowance represented a bonus, rather than a compensation for lack of skill and experience. The gamble nearly came off as Welsh Pet held a slight lead at the last hurdle and was only headed in the run-in, Stipend winning by three-quarters of a length.

3

JACK REARDON

Jack Reardon was one who repudiated George Lambton's doubts as to the lack of characters in the modern racing world. By coincidence he served his time with George Lambton, for whom he had the greatest admiration both as a trainer and a man. Before taking up training Jack had been a good jump jockey, winning a war-time Grand National on Vermouth in 1916. Of all the horses Jack rode, the dearest to his heart was Captain Dreyfus, a spectacular front-running 'chaser on whom he won many races.

I first met Jack Reardon some years before the war through Tom Masson, and it was Jack for whom I had my first ride over fences, on Tremolite at Sandown. It nearly proved my last as Tremolite gave me a crashing fall at the fence down the hill, because I could not hold him and went into the obstacle too fast. A small, neat man, always impeccably dressed, Jack had a sharp, alert face, with rather a prominent nose, his general appearance giving the impression that he might be a stage comedian. Indeed, Geoff Harbord used to say he reminded him of the ventriloquist Harry Tate's boy. Jack trained at Ermyn Lodge, which is just off the Headley road at Epsom, a short way down a grass track, which was a Roman road. It was a beautifully kept establishment, with about a dozen boxes and a paddock big enough to work horses round the perimeter, in which he had some hurdles. He seldom had more than half a dozen horses in training, most of which he owned wholly or partially himself. ''I've got eight horses this season and it's worrying me to death,'' he once observed. The stable was run entirely for betting and Jack would leave out no detail in planning a coup, for which he was prepared to wait as long as he thought fit. His horses were always perfectly trained and turned out, for he was a perfectionist in every way.

Jack was a heavy bettor himself and made a fortune out of racing, sufficient to enable him to buy a house in the West Indies to which, later in life, he retired during the winter. He was a modest winner and wonderful loser: once when a coup had gone wrong on a horse called Little Barrington which Brian Swift, then an apprentice, 'did', he replied to the condolences of a friend: "It might have been worse, I only had five thousand on him." Jack enjoyed telling stories against himself and was a most entertaining raconteur. With his horses he kept his cards close to his chest and no-one quite knew what he was up to. I once rode a horse for him in an amateur race at Salisbury, which I felt was only running in order to get him handicapped, as he blew up before the end of the race and Jack expressed no displeasure at his defeat or about the way I rode him, despite the horse starting favourite. He did not mind throwing away £100 or so on an unfancied horse, as a blind. On one occasion he borrowed a horse from Ron Smyth, to try one of his own, on which he intended to have a gamble if the trial came out right. "I didn't know the name of his horse, he didn't know the name of mine," Ron related to me. The gallop came out right and Ron arranged for Jack to back the horse for him when it ran. It was beaten and Ron paid up. Some weeks later Jack remarked to Ron, "I never cashed your cheque, but I'm going to put your money on when next he runs." This time the horse won, at a more lucrative price than if he had done the first time when, perhaps, he was 'unlucky'.

Like all good gamblers Jack knew that the essence of success is in taking a calculated risk at a fair price. One winter the weather in the Beckhampton area had been particularly bad, lasting late into spring, while conditions at Epsom were much better. Jack had a two-year-old called Saucy Boy, whom he had tried to be pretty useful, so he decided to send him to Bath, ridden by Harry Sprague, then an apprentice. Fred Darling regularly used to win nearly every early two-year-old race at Bath and Salisbury, where he liked to bring out his good youngsters in order to give them an easy task as an introduction to racing. Ridden by Gordon Richards, they invariably started hot favourites. Jack formed the opinion that, in view of training conditions at Beckhampton, it would be impossible for Fred's horses to be fully fit, so that in taking him on he would have something in hand on this account, and had a good bet on Saucy Boy. He had great faith in Harry Sprague as a jockey and on all counts his judgment was vindicated as Saucy Boy won, beating Fred's

44

runner, Phaetonia, a short head. Phaetonia's later form proved that she was superior to Saucy Boy, confirming the nicety of Jack's assessment. Jack was an exacting but just critic of jockeys. "These little hands can hold him, so what's wrong with you," he observed to a rider of whom one of his horses took charge. Jack's favourite jockey under N.H. Rules was Gerry Hardy, a particularly able rider who unfortunately had to give up as a result of a bad fall. Gerry complained about Jack that, win or lose, he always found some fault with his riding, to get a rise out of him. Once, having carried out his orders to perfection, Gerry said on returning to scale: "Well, what did I do wrong this time?" At once the reply came: "You went to the post too fast." Sadly, when he retired, Jack's mind deteriorated and he died a few years later in 1974.

4

KAMI, CLONCARRIG AND THE GRAND NATIONAL

One morning early in 1947 I was in Tom Masson's flat at Lewes after riding work. He had in his stable two French 'chasers, Kami and Vol au Vent, which had been sent over to England in the hope of a buyer being found for them. Kami had run well before falling at the thirteenth fence in the previous year's Grand National and, ridden by the French jockey Bobby Bates, had won a 'chase at Plumpton on New Year's Day of 1947, carrying 12st. 7lbs. Vol au Vent had finished second in a 'chase at Windsor to a pretty good horse belonging to Jakie Astor called The Diver. Both Kami and Vol au Vent had good form in France.

"I wish we could find someone to buy Kami and let you ride him in the National," Tom remarked to me. "He doesn't want a French jockey sitting up his neck at Liverpool; he's not a big horse and you'd suit him. They could buy Vol au Vent as well, if they wanted, and the package deal would be good value." I said, "There's only one person I can think of and I've no idea if he's still around. He's called Sir Allan Gordon-Smith, and I rode a point-to-point winner for one of his daughters before the war. He used to live at Goodwood, so might be in the telephone book." We looked to see if this was so and found him listed at his old address, so I put a call through on chance, finding him there. "You probably don't remember me, but I rode Black Grape at the Crawley and Horsham point-to-point," I said. "Oh yes, I remember you well, and I'm glad to hear from you again," he replied. I went on: "I've rung to ask if you'd be interested in a horse that might run well in the Cheltenham Gold Cup and would have a good chance in the 'National."

"Would you ride him?"

"Yes, I'd love to."

"Well, I'll have him if he passes the vet."

I then explained the package deal and he ended by deciding to take both horses. In this way began a happy friendship and association, which lasted until Sir Allan's death at the age of seventy in 1951.

Sir Allan was one of the most delightful characters I have known. He loved life, sport and people, was seldom without a smile on his face and a light in his eye, and, while a hard-working and successful business-man, he made one feel that giving and sharing enjoyment was more important than making money. He always wore a monocle, which lent him a certain panache, was a warm and generous host, a good winner and met defeat with philosophical cheerfulness. His business was Smith's Clocks and Accessories, of which he was the head. Sir Allan had come into racing through the coursing world, in which he had gained fame by twice winning the Waterloo Cup, with Golden Seal and Golden Surprise. In this circle he met the trainer, Jack (later Sir Jack) Jarvis, also a coursing enthusiast and likewise owner of two Waterloo Cup winners, Genial Nobleman and Jovial Judge, after whom he named a useful 'chaser he owned, which was trained by his brother-in-law, Tom Leader.

Having won the most important of all coursing events twice, the idea of trying to win the Grand National appealed to Sir Allan. Kami and Vol au Vent duly passed the vet and became Sir Allan's property. Kami was the most delightful horse, a dark bay gelding, full of quality and more like a flat racer than a 'chaser. He stood barely 16 hands and looked on the small side, as he was rather narrow to follow and slightly built for a jumper, but had beautiful, clean limbs, a fine shoulder, good depth through the heart, a lovely intelligent gazelle-like head, with perceptibly lop ears, and a sweet temperament. By an odd coincidence he came from the stud of M. Evremonde de St. Alary, for whom Victor Gilpin had trained at Newmarket when I was with him.

No sooner had Sir Allan acquired Kami and Vol au Vent than a cold spell of exceptional severity set in. All racing ceased and training was reduced to walking and trotting. Between January 21st and March 15th not a single meeting was held. Thus Kami's first engagement became the Grand National on March 28th. With fast work impossible at Lewes, we took Kami regularly to work on the sands at Bracklesham Bay, between East Wittering and Selsey, on the Sussex coast. This afforded a fine stretch of sand for several miles. After unboxing the horses we walked and jogged them for a bit, cantered down along the edge of the sea where the sand was wet just after the tide had ebbed, and then galloped back. It provided quite good going, as the surface was smooth and level, but below the top two inches the ground was rock hard, so much so that a horse which Tom Masson and I owned between us, Insolate, who was one of Kami's work companions, developed sore shins. Luckily Kami was unaffected and Tom was able to keep him pretty fit. It was not an enjoyable form of riding. Apart from the bitterly cold weather, the wind blew sand into everything, eyes, ears, nose and clothing, and we were soaked with spray thrown up from puddles of sea water through which we galloped. A careful watch had to be kept against horses getting cracked heels. The fitness of horses was not the only problem; jockeys, too, had to keep themselves in condition. This entailed such tedious occupations as doing exercises, running and manual labour. In this way I, like others, managed as best I could.

I had confined my riding under N.H. Rules almost exclusively to hurdle races, and was not keen to take the chance of being put out of action before the 'National, so my only ride in public before the day was on Gremlin in the Imperial Cup, in which he was unplaced. It was probably a wise precaution, as in the steeplechases run during the period immediately following the long hold-up of racing, an unusually high number of horses fell or were pulled up. Apart from the factor of lack of fitness among horses, the fences in those days were of pre-war stiffness, being appreciably more difficult to jump than they are today. The Aintree fences are now bevelled at the top away from the take-off side and, in the case of the plain fences, have gorse aprons in front of them, which was not so in those days, when horses often fell through taking off too close to them.

The portents to completing the course in the 'National that year were not encouraging. On the Thursday, sixteen horses contested the Stanley 'Chase, of which two finished, both having fallen and been remounted. On the Friday, of the nineteen runners in the Becher 'Chase, no more than five finished; while in the Foxhunters' Chase only two of the five starters completed the course, the winner falling and being remounted. Since there were 57 horses due to start in the 'National, all of which eventually went to the post, the outlook was not conducive to an easy night's sleep. 1947 was the first year in living memory that the 'National was run on a Saturday, instead of the traditional Friday, and I have always felt that the decline in the prestige of the race dates from this change. Obviously, other factors brought this about, chiefly the intro-duction of new, rich steeplechase prizes and the vast increase of the prize money for the Cheltenham Gold Cup. Nevertheless the change from the Friday to Saturday started the rot, because it disrupted the established habits of the racing world, did away with the traditional 'National-Night Dinner – who wants to be stuck in Liverpool on Sunday morning? – and brought the race up against the rival, local attraction of football.

It is impossible for those who did not live in the pre-war era to understand the impact of the 'National on the sporting world in those times. To start with, while the Great Sefton 'Chase, was about the only other 'chase worth £1,000 or more, the 'National prize money was almost as large as that of The Derby. For the jumping world the 'National was the one supreme event, and the ambition of every owner, trainer and rider was to win it. The Cheltenham Gold Cup gradually grew in importance, but for the whole of the period between the two wars it never approached the status of the 'National. Every new star to appear in the steeplechasing firmament was assessed and discussed in the light of his likely chance in a future 'National. The idea that this race might not be considered as the horse's eventual objective was unthinkable. This interest and enthusiasm was reflected in the press, among backers, bookmakers and the general public. Every sporting newspaper and magazine had its Grand National number and even such staid publications as *The Illustrated London News* gave the race a generous coverage, both before and after. To obtain a room at Liverpool or nearby for the meeting, it was necessary to book a year ahead. Professional racing men made permanent arrangements for accommodation, either in hotels, rooms, or by renting private houses. Socially, no racing man or woman would dream of not attending the 'National meeting.

As the day of the race approached, the excitement built up. Among those involved directly, tension grew almost to breaking point. In the jockeys' room the atmosphere was something akin to that among soldiers and air crews about to go into action: we would wish each other good luck, experienced riders would give a word of encouragement to those taking part in the race for the first time, valets would wish their jockeys a safe return, and old hands who had hung up their boots would come into the jockeys' room, which in those days they were allowed to do, to shake hands with friends who were riding. Spectators wanting to be sure of a place on the stands during the big race had to be there well beforehand, unless they had access to a private box or a reserved seat. As he paraded before the race, it was an awe-inspiring sight for a jockey to look up at the dense mass of humanity on the stands, from which emanated a hum of suppressed excitement, soon to swell and burst into a roar as the gate went up, dying down as the race progressed and rising in a crescendo to its climax as the winner passed the post. After the war, as the merit of horses competing deteriorated, the quality of the meeting began to fall and the crowds to thin out, more and more being content to watch the race on television, but for the first year or two after the war, much of the old atmosphere remained.

A number of jockeys, professional and amateur, used to stay near the racecourse rather than in Liverpool itself. It was more convenient for riding work in the morning, and for getting to the racecourse on 'National day. Most trainers gave their runners a sharp canter on the morning of the race and I always felt better for a ride before racing: it stimulated circulation, cleared the lungs and helped to calm nerves. Sometimes other trainers would ask me to work horses, perhaps flat racers as I was light, which I enjoyed. Early morning on a racecourse the day of an important race has a special atmosphere of bustle and excitement. Owners, trainers and journalists are out to see the competitors for the big event, or other horses in which they are interested, jockeys are busy riding work or changing mounts, horses flash by singly or in twos and threes, and views are exchanged on how they look and move, and about their chances later in the day. Together with Bob Turnell and a number of other jockeys, I used to stay in a house a few hundred yards from the course, and this time Jean accompanied me. We woke to a damp, cold, foggy, uninviting morning, which presaged anything but pleasant conditions for the race. However, Kami moved well in his early work and there was always hope that the weather would improve. It didn't. A fine rain settled in, the mist obscured visibility over most of the course and the going deteriorated, so much so that the Stewards considered cutting out two fences, but in the end decided to leave them in. In view of the risk of Kami spreading a plate, which the exigencies of heavy going can bring about, he was shod with tips all round, as opposed to full shoes. In his gallant attempt to win the 'National of 1929 under 12st. 7lbs, Easter Hero, who finished second to Gregalach, was much hampered by a spread plate, which contributed to his defeat. Another precaution we took was to fit Kami with a breast-girth, to prevent the saddle going back; this is liable to happen at Aintree, where the fences are wide and high and tend to pull the girths back as a horse brushes through the top. There are enough hazards in the 'National without adding to them through lack of attention to details of equipment.

When the riders were called out for the race, the weather was no better. Under the most agreeable conditions, riding in the 'National is daunting, even to the experienced and mentally tough, let alone those of nervous disposition. With the huge field, heavy going, unpleasant weather and the ominous number of horses failing to complete the course in the preceding steeplechases, the prospect was far from encouraging. It was a relief to end the tension of that apprehensive interval between weighing out and leaving the jockeys' room for the paddock, but on seeing so many horses in the parade ring that they had to walk round in a double circle, I was little short of terrified. My feelings must have been evident, as Sir Allan remarked when I joined him and Tom Masson in the ring, "You don't look very well," which could have been an understatement. Having had excellent results from a couple of benzedrine tablets during the war, I took a similar dose about half an hour before the race; but I failed to appreciate that the effect on a stomach unburdened by food for some two days during the stresses of active warfare was not the same as that based on an ample and regular peacetime diet, with the result that the tablets had no effect whatever until about seven o'clock that evening, when I felt like staying up all night. However, I assured Sir Allan that I had never felt fitter, adding that my complexion, which he afterwards told me matched the predominantly green hue of his racing colours, was due to the raw coldness of the afternoon. I'd doubt if he believed me. As is usually the case, I felt better when I was in the saddle and after cantering to the post. Kami gave me a good feel and seemed at ease on the heavy ground.

Walking round at the starting gate I found myself beside Dan Moore, who in 1938 on Royal Danieli had lost the 'National narrowly to Bruce Hobbs on Battleship. He was riding the second favourite, Revelry, a huge, rather common horse who, ridden by Dan, later won the Irish National. Beside Revelry, Kami must have seemed like a child's pony. As he looked down on him, Dan remarked to me: "I wouldn't ride that round here for all the tea in China." Revelry fell at the first fence. The observation did not depress me, as I had confidence in Kami; I was more concerned as to how we were going to sort ourselves out in the huge field.

There are various theories about riding in the 'National: to be up with the leaders and clear of the bulk of the runners; to keep to the inside, thus saving ground; to take the middle of the course, where the drops on the landing side of the fences – now modified – were then appreciably less pronounced than on the inside and the outside; to concentrate on completing the first circuit, no matter where you go, before considering the finer aspects of tactics; or making no fixed plans, riding the race as it comes up. The stable had backed Kami each way at long odds, so the first objective was to get round. He had a reasonably light weight, stayed well and was a good jumper, but being lightly built would come off worse if he collided with other horses. It was agreed, therefore, that if possible I would lay up among or not far off the leaders, and try to keep clear of other runners. I lined up about the middle, towards the inside rather than the outside. The unusually large number of runners stretched right across the course, and in the section in which I found myself, we were pressed together like sardines in a tin. So tightly were the horses on the outside of this group pressing in on us that, when the gate went up, about half a dozen of us could not move for what seemed several seconds. To make matters worse, Kami, being small and light, was squeezed back out of the line by the horses on either side of him. By the time he started the leaders were what seemed about a hundred yards ahead, and our plan to be near or among them had sunk without trace. I was mortified, but there was nothing to be done, except keep going and avoid trouble. Kami brought me some cheer by jumping the first fence impeccably, and as the next few fences and then Becher's were coped with in the same fluent manner, the hope arose that at least he might complete the course. In fact, in the whole race he never put a foot wrong. Only once did he give me a fright: on the second circuit at one of the early fences, he met it wrong and stood so far back that I thought he was sure to fall. The fear was unjustified, for he cleared the fence with ease. In the mist and rain it was impossible to see how the race was developing, but steadily we passed horse after horse, some with riders, others without. I remember the late Derek Jackson (Professor D. A. Jackson, OBE DFC AFC MA Bsc FRS) calling a word of encouragement to me as I passed him. By the time we reached the racecourse, heading for the finish, I could see that there were only three horses left in front of us. The two leaders were still a long way ahead and I had no idea who they were, but the horse immediately before me was coming back to us fast and as we started to make the bend approaching the last two fences, I could see that it was Prince Regent. The gallant old horse, now twelve and carrying top weight of 12st. 7lbs., was dead beat. The heavy going was an additional handicap to him and only his noble spirit was keeping him going. We passed him some way before the last two fences and I realised that we had only to stand up to finish in the first three.

The leader, which proved to be Caughoo, ridden by Eddie Dempsey and carrying only 10st., had gone beyond recall; bar a fall he had won. The second, Lough Conn, with a pound more on his back, was still some twenty lengths ahead of us, so I concentrated everything on getting safely over the final two fences rather than on attempting the impossible task of catching the pair ahead of me. In the fluent style in which he had crossed all the earlier fences of this formidable course, Kami dealt with the last two, and all our worries were over. I kept Kami going by swinging my whip without touching him, and got within four lengths of Lough Conn, who had made much of the early running and tired after the last fence, but Caughoo had twenty lengths to spare over him to give his Irish owner, Mr. J.J. McDowell, and his trainer, H. McDowell, an easy victory. The brave and noble Prince Regent finished fourth, nineteen horses completing the course, some having been remounted.

Though failing in our main objective to win the 'National, we had succeeded in attaining our secondary target, that of being placed, and Sir Allan was delighted. The immediate reaction was mental and physical exhaustion, but I soon revived, due doubtless to Tom Masson giving me half a glass of neat whisky after I had weighed in.

Kami was then put by for an attempt on the 'National the following year. He did exceptionally well during the summer and we were hopeful that he would go two better next time. It was not to be. He reappeared in a three-mile handicap 'chase at Kempton, in which he stood too far back at the open ditch by the stables, landing on top of the fence. He did not come down, but lost a lot of ground and finished last of eight, the race being won by Roimond, a top class 'chaser owned by Lord Bicester, trained by George Beeby and ridden by Dick Black, by then a professional. I felt that Kami was a bit too fresh, as a result of which he did not pay the meticulous care to the fence which he usually did.

He next ran at Lingfield, where he slipped up on the flat rounding the bend by the stands. He then ran well at Windsor; though last of seven, he carried 12st. 1lb, jumped perfectly and was not fully wound up. Kami's next race was the Troytown Handicap 'Chase at Lingfield. The going was officially described as good, but the surface was greasy, rain having fallen after a dry spell. As he took off at the first fence Kami slipped, crashed it and came down. He got up, but I saw at once that his leg was broken above the knee and realised bitterly that this was the end. A few minutes later he was shot. I felt his death deeply, he was such a gentle, courageous horse and I owed so much to him.

Sir Allan Gordon-Smith was never a man to bow to adversity or tragedy. Though deeply saddened by the death of Kami, he determined to try again to win the Grand National, and asked me to look out for a horse to do so. The bloodstock sales revealed nothing that appealed, nor did investigation among private dealers; but one day an idea struck me. At the Liverpool November meeting I had seen a horse win one of the races over part of the 'National course, who both as an individual and by his performance left a lasting impression. I can still recall the picture of him standing in the paddock, about to be mounted before the race: a big, powerful, rangy, brown horse, combining strength with quality, gazing towards the racecourse over the crowd surrounding the paddock, proud, calm and confident. He had a bold, honest head, and a large eye, the expression courageous and kind. In the race he jumped magnificently, sprinted away from the last fence and won easily. At the time I thought, "If ever I saw a 'National horse, that's the one." His name was Cloncarrig and he was trained in Ireland. In our search for a horse, Cloncarrig never occurred to me, probably because I took it for granted that had he been for sale one of the prominent owners, such as Lord Bicester, would have snapped him up. But as time passed and no suitable prospect appeared, I suddenly remembered him and said to Sir Allan: "I do know just the horse, but don't expect he's for sale," going on to tell him about Cloncarrig. He was thrilled with the idea of the horse and said: "I'll get in touch with an old pal of mine, Spencer Freeman, who lives in Ireland, and ask him to find out if he can be bought. Spencer and I worked together in the war and I can rely on him absolutely to discover everything about the horse."

A day or so later he telephoned to say that he had spoken to Spencer Freeman, who had contacted the owner and secured an option on Cloncarrig at a reasonable price. It was arranged that Tom Masson and I, accompanied by John Carless the veterinary surgeon, should fly over to see Cloncarrig and, if we approved, buy him. In those days it was necessary to have a passport to get into Ireland. Jean and I were staying the night at the Berkeley Hotel in London, I think because I was catching an early flight. Just as I got into bed, I realised that I had left my passport at Pelham House, in Cuckfield, where we had moved from Simmonds Farm in 1946. There was no option but to get up and go to fetch it, which I did; at least it was better than arriving at the airport with no passport. Spencer Freeman laid on the whole operation. Spencer Freeman was a charming man, with a quiet, dignified manner, but not without a hint of humour, his white hair and tactful phraseology giving the impression of a Minister of the Crown as much as a business man of standing. He was a master of organisation, efficiency and attention to detail: the prosperity of racing in Ireland today is largely due to him, as a result of his conceiving the idea of The Irish Sweeps Derby, putting it into effect with the utmost skill and diplomacy, and thus bringing Ireland to the forefront of international racing, the country previously having been a backwater of the sport. I do not believe that his work has received the recognition it deserves.

We stayed the night with Spencer Freeman, as we were to see the horse early the following morning. The perfect host, Spencer was also the perfect showman. The previous year I had written for *The Observer* a description of the Grand National from the rider's aspect, which was something of a journalistic coup in those days, as it had never been done before; and after dinner Spencer showed us the film of the 'National and, as a commentary, read out my piece, blending the two with masterly precision. Cloncarrig was trained at Craddoxtown House, Naas, not far from Dublin, by Joe Osborne, a pleasant, cheery man, who had been an amateur rider. He told me that he had once ridden the great Easter Hero, when the horse was unknown. He said the horse pulled like a train and gave him a dreadful ride. I think it must have been on the training ground, as I can find no record of Osborne having ridden Easter Hero in public. Cloncarrig confirmed the impression he made on me when I first saw him. He was a truly magnificent type; if he could be faulted it was that he was a shade light through the loin and a little long in his pasterns. I cantered him round the field and found him a powerful ride, with a long sweeping stride, giving me the feeling that he was a steeplechaser of the highest order. He had an interesting pedigree: in tail female line of descent he traced to Sceptre, one of the greatest racemares in Turf history and to whom he bore a distinct resemblance. John Carless passed Cloncarrig sound, the sale was ratified and the horse came over to England and into Tom Masson's yard.

I rode Cloncarrig out regularly, working him by himself, as he pulled fairly hard in company. He thrived, but suffered from chronic red-worm and disliked the cold. The red-worm was kept under control with treatment, and the warm climate of Sussex suited him. We planned to run him in the National Hunt Handicap 'Chase at Cheltenham and then in the 'National. Cloncarrig was fit when he arrived from Ireland, so did not need much work. The undulations of downland training grounds are exacting, and if horses are given the work which they need when trained on flat gallops they soon reach a state in which "you can read a newspaper through them" as Geoff Harbord used to say. Geoff, a friend from pre-war days when we shared Clarehaven Cottage at Newmarket, used to write on hunting and racing for *The Tatler*. A fine horseman and a good man to hounds, he had been an instructor at Weedon, a bookmaker and a serious punter.

I was not too confident of doing justice to Cloncarrig in a race; I was light and did not have the strength of most steeplechase riders, who would thus be better adapted to control and balance a big, powerful horse such as Cloncarrig. A few, exceptional, light riders, such as Martin Molony and Stan Mellor, are able to ride horses of this type as well as – or better than – anyone, but most top jump jockeys are bigger and more powerfully built. So it proved in the race. After going really well in the lead and giving me a wonderful feeling, Cloncarrig hit the fence after the water and shot me off. I was humiliated and when I met Sir Allan after the race, I urged him to let a more suitable jockey, preferably Martin Molony, who had ridden the horse successfully before, ride him in the 'National; but Sir Allan wouldn't hear of it, insisting that I continue to partner the horse.

In contrast to the dreadful conditions in which the previous year's race took place, the Grand National of 1948 was run on perfect going in warm, sunny weather. There were 43 starters, of which Cloncarrig, who carried 10st. 13lbs, was joint third favourite. We began auspiciously. Cloncarrig broke well and was among the leaders at the first fence, which he jumped so cleanly and smoothly that it felt as if the obstacle was no more than a hurdle. This fine jump took him into the lead, where he remained, galloping easily, taking no more than a nice hold and jumping immaculately till he turned for home nearing the end of the first circuit. He must have thought that he was heading for the finish, his former experience of the course having entailed going round only once, because he suddenly took a ferocious hold of his bit and virtually ran away with me. I found it impossible to steady him, so that we came into the 13th fence unbalanced and too fast. He hit it fairly hard, and though it appeared to make no difference to him it did to me. I was precipitated ignominiously out of the saddle and out of the race. Had we completed the course I am sure he would have won.

Cloncarrig's next engagement was the first running of the Golden Miller 'Chase at Cheltenham, over four miles. Being a new and valuable event, it created considerable interest and publicity, drawing a good entry of high class horses, among them several prominent in the Grand National. Despite my having fallen off Cloncarrig at Aintree, Sir Allan insisted on me riding the horse again. When Cloncarrig came over from Ireland I asked Martin Molony the best way to ride him. He replied, "he loves a kick going into his fences." Most steeplechasers jump best when

56

urged into the obstacles by pressure of the rider's legs, which ensures that they have the necessary momentum to jump fast and get quickly away from the obstacle on landing. The exception is a horse who has been schooled in France, where jockeys sit perfectly still and leave everything to the horse. If a French-trained 'chaser is kicked into a fence, he is liable to be confused and perhaps fail to take off at all. Bearing in mind Martin Molony's advice, I rode Cloncarrig into his fences in each of my first two races on him; and while he jumped magnificently at all the fences he met in his stride, when he met one out of his stride he made no effort to put himself right, so hit it hard. He was powerful enough to get away with it, but the impact dislodged me – security in the saddle was never my strong point over fences. This time Tom Masson decided that the wisest procedure was to leave the horse alone to jump as he pleased, and not to drive him into his fences; on the principle that although he might not gain so much ground jumping, he would be less likely to make a mistake and, if he did so, the force of impact would not be so violent as would be the case if he was travelling faster. In order to try to make Cloncarrig easier to steady, Tom Masson put a chain snaffle on him for this race. The bit had worked admirably on a hard-pulling horse called Big Ben, whom I rode for him before the war, but it did not suit Cloncarrig: every time I took a pull at him he swung his head to one side and refused to be steadied, so I was forced to leave him alone to run as he liked, without trying to steady him.

The runners included the Grand National winner of 1947, Lovely Cottage; Freebooter, winner of the 'National in 1950, who fell early in the race; and Zahia, who was galloping strongly in the 'National – her previous race – in second place at the last fence but one, when her ride mistook the course and she ran out. Cloncarrig was always going well, moved up to join Zahia at the last fence and went on to win by three lengths. Since he was meeting Zahia on 3lbs. worse terms than at Liverpool, and the mare looked likely to win when she ran out, Cloncarrig was pretty sure to have won the 'National, had I not parted company with him. The Golden Miller 'Chase was my last winner over fences, in fact, I had made up my mind that it was to be my last ride over fences, but I took one more – in a soldiers' race at Sandown, because Ivor Anthony could not find a rider for a horse belonging to Sir Humphrey de Trafford; I was qualified to ride and it was a safe jumper. I had a good ride, finishing about fourth or fifth, but was not sorry to be giving up. I was getting old for steeplechasing and my nerve was 'on the amber' as they say in the game, which is a bad portent for safety and success.

Cloncarrig continued to race for Sir Allan, winning the Golden Miller 'Chase in 1949, the Becher 'Chase and other races; and after the latter's death was bought by Bill (Sir William) Dugdale, giving his owner some good rides and eventually being retired.

Sir Allan was unlucky not to win the Grand National of 1950 with Cloncarrig, whom he then had in partnership with Mr. Jack Olding. The horse had been operated on for his wind successfully and was as good as ever. Ridden by Bob Turnell, he came to the last fence but one pulling over Freebooter. So certain a winner did he look that a friend of Jack Olding turned to him and said, "You can't lead in a 'National winner wearing a soft hat, Jack; here, take my bowler," and as he handed over the hat Cloncarrig hit the fence and came down. Bob Turnell blamed himself for riding into the fence too confidently, instead of steadying him and making sure he got over safely; but Cloncarrig was going so strongly and was so safe a jumper, even if he hit a fence every now and then, that he was being unduly critical of himself. The fact that Cloncarrig had 11st. 9lbs, whereas in 1948 he had only 10st. 13lbs, indicates that he almost certainly would have won that 'National had I stayed on him.

Sir Allan Gordon-Smith's partner in Cloncarrig, Jack Olding, was prominent in the road construction business. He was a keen racing man with little or no technical knowledge of the game, looking upon it purely as a relaxation. His flat racers were trained by Atty Persse and after the latter's death by Noel Cannon, and his jumpers, except for Cloncarrig, were with Ivor Anthony. Outwardly a cheery, easy going character, ruddy faced, of medium height and build, I suspect he was tough and astute in business. He was always accompanied by Reg MacCooey, a retired CID officer, who acted as Jack's ADC. On the racecourse they were usually joined by a party of friends at the table reserved for Jack in the restaurant.

Reg MacCooey, who owned the odd racehorse himself, had many interesting stories from his days as a detective. He once told me that as a young man working under a senior officer, one of his first cases in which he was involved was that of the murderer Landru. They were inspecting Landru's business premises – he was a butcher – and Reg had his back to his superior, who called to him: "Have a look at this," and Reg turned round to see him holding up by its long black hair the dripping head of a woman, which he had pulled out of a vat of salted water holding joints of meat. MacCooey passed straight out.

I bought a couple of horses for Jack Olding, a handsome but moderate hurdler and a pretty good flat-racer called Rose Argent. The latter, a beautiful brown colt by Owen Tudor out of Zepherin, came from his breeder, Major Charles Reynard MC, a keen and successful breeder despite the restraint of modest means. Charles Reynard was a good judge of conformation and had a fine knowledge and understanding of pedigrees, upon which subject we had much discussion and correspondence. He was a believer in judicious and carefully balanced breeding, and a sound tail female line. On these principles Rose Argent's pedigree was based, as he was inbred 3×3 to Pharos, with a more remote duplication of Gainsborough, and traced to the Oaks winner, Rose of England, through a full sister to The St. Leger winner Chulmleigh. I cannot remember the price of Rose Argent, but it was not excessive, and he proved well worth the money, winning the Houghton Stakes at two and the Atlanta Stakes at three, among several other races, and gained some lucrative placings, being seldom out of the first three. At the end of his three-year-old season he was sold to go to Australia as a stallion, becoming the sire of that fine steeplechaser, Crisp, who came to England and was unluckily beaten by Red Rum in the Grand National of 1973, carrying top weight.

5

PEOPLE AND EVENTS

We did not stay long at Simmonds Farm. It was too small and the landlord wanted a tenant more interested in farming than racing, so we decided to look for another house, finding one at Cuckfield called Pelham House. It was pleasant, with a garden, cottage and paddock, and faced the main road which ran through the village. Also in the village were Bob and Angela Fox, whose youngest son Robert, called after his godfather Robert Morley, was a godson of mine as well. Bob, who died at a tragically young age from a tumour on the brain, was Robert Morley's theatrical agent.

We all gathered at Robert Fox's christening, the party including the journalist Godfrey Winn and Robert Morley's son Sheridan, then a boy in his teens. At that stage of his life Sheridan was rather plump, and Godfrey Winn unkindly remarked: "Robert, your boy's figure is a disaster," to which Robert replied: "The trouble with you, Godfrey, is that young boys' figures have been your disaster." At this Godfrey Winn turned scarlet, gave a squeal of indignation and fled from the scene.

I had many friends in Sussex, having worked with the trainer Victor Gilpin at Michel Grove near Findon for two or three years before the war. Among them were Miles and Leila Manton (Lord and Lady Manton), who lived at Plumpton Place, where we first met Robert Morley, at dinner one evening. Also dining was Lord Snowdon's father, Mr. Armstrong-Jones. Like me, Robert Morley had undergone the rigours of that 'seminary of sound learning and religious education', Wellington College, Berkshire, which always remained one of the unhappiest experiences of his life. In racing, we shared a more agreeable common interest. Robert was, however, of a different political hue to the assembled company, being a Socialist. As the evening progressed, we fell into a political discussion which, while friendly, became extremely warm, Jean in particular castigating Robert for maintaining double standards, by staying in luxury and eating Miles's good food and drinking his excellent wine and brandy, while purporting to be a true Socialist. So effective was her attack that Robert was finally silenced; and when we got home at about one in the morning, Mr. Armstrong-Jones telephoned to congratulate her on the way in which she had demolished Robert's arguments. Despite this we remained friends with Robert (who died in 1992) and occasionally met on the racecourse. In fact, at one time we both had a horse with the same trainer, Evan Williams, when the latter was at Kingsclere, before he retired to become a Master of Hounds in Ireland. The horse, named after a play in which Robert was acting, The Gloomy Sentry, carried his 'yellow, blue bird's eye cap' to victory at least once. Over the years Robert owned a number of winners, without spending an undue amount. Some years after the period covered by this book, we went round to see Robert in his dressing room, having been to one of his plays, which I think was The Little Hut. During the conversation I mentioned that we had an exceptionally promising yearling colt called Brigadier Gerard, who might go on to win The Two Thousand Guineas. In due course this came to pass, after which Robert, an inveterate punter, remarked to a friend: "I'm furious with John Hislop. He came into my dressing room told me he'd got a yearling that would win The Two Thousand Guineas, and I thought he was off his head, so took no notice."

We had a happy time at Pelham House. There were plenty of friends in the neighbourhood, it was convenient for racing and close to Lewes, where our horses were trained by Tom Masson, for whom I used to ride work. The climate was mild: we only once turned on the central heating, to see if it worked, and found it unbearably hot. Futhermore our elder son, Ian Anthony, was born while we lived there on June 16th, 1949. He was given his second name after Anthony Mildmay (Lord Mildmay), one of his godfathers and a friend of my pre-war race riding days. Among other old friends were John and Patricia Abergavenny (Lord and Lady Abergavenny), Roddy and Ursula Pratt (Lord and Lady Roderick Pratt), Jack and Joan Dennis, Peter and Phil Duncanson and Phil and Val Kindersley; as a result, we had a pleasant social life. When we first went to Pelham House petrol rationing was in force and traffic on the main road immediately beside us was light; but when rationing ceased the traffic became unbearable and we decided to move. We found a buyer for our house, luckily, as it was by no means structurally sound; being built on clay, the foundations moving according to the weather, causing cracks to come and go. The elderly lady who bought it was more concerned about the accommodation which the house offered, particularly a separate apartment within it, than surveyors' reports and, after seeing it, made up her mind straight away that she would have it. The sale went through and we found ourselves looking for somewhere to live.

For a time we stayed as paying guests with my mother-in-law at Letcombe Regis, while we looked for another house. We intended to stay near Lewes, so as to be within reach of Tom Masson's yard in the town; and we wanted a property with some land, where we could keep a brood mare, since I had become interested in breeding and viewed it as an occupation when my race riding days were over. We looked at various houses, but none were suitable. One seemed possible, but I had an odd premonition against it and rather to Jean's irritation, for I kept finding fault with every house we looked at, turned it down. I heard later that part of it subsided. One day Jean remarked that there was a property for sale near Newbury, on the Highclere side, called East Woodhay House, owned by Herbie Pretyman, an ex-naval officer and keen racing man for whom I rode a couple of winners on his horse Maisey Hampton. It was bigger than we thought of buying, but as we had nothing to do that day we decided to go to look at it for fun. When I saw it I liked it straight away, and decided to buy it. Though it was a larger property than we could afford to run, consisting of 80 acres including a stud farm, it had a great advantage from our point of view. There was a ten-year lease on the stud farm held by Herbert Blagrave, owner of the adjoining Harwood Stud, now the Gainsborough Stud, which meant that the expense of running the stud was off our hands for the time being, and the fact that there was a lease on the stud kept down the price, few people other than ourselves, wished to buy a stud farm without a house to go with it, or a house with someone else having a lease on the land. We agreed a price, £20,000, which today reads a gift, since the property included three cottages, as well as a stud yard, isolation boxes and railed paddocks. East Woodhay House, originally Georgian, was burned down in about 1901 and rebuilt in what might be described as 'Newmarket Edwardian' style, but was not unpleasing, comfortable inside and we spent many happy years there, during which our second son, Andrew, was born on January 15th, 1951. Over the years we added improvements: a single apartment converted from a stable, a hard tennis court and swimming pool, boarded and boundary fencing, and we were able to have a right of way across the park extinguished. The property is now occupied by Juliet Reed, who runs it as a partly commercial stud and has done much, both to the main house and the fencing. The sale went through without a hitch; the Pretymans could not have been nicer people to deal with. It was a big step for us, but proved well worth while, though sometimes the financial aspect worried me, having been brought up in the Victorian precepts of never living beyond one's income or having an overdraft. However, we survived; and when, years after, Peter O'Sullevan asked me whether the comparative affluence which Brigadier Gerard brought us had made any difference to my style of life, I answered: "Only that I can afford to live as I've been doing for the last twenty years."

About the time we moved to East Woodhay House, my old friend Geoff Harbord and his wife Daultie came to live quite near, at Clatford Mill, a few miles south of Newbury. I first met Geoff when I was a learner in the racing stable of Victor Gilpin, at Clarehaven in Newmarket, before the war. He was a friend of Victor and then single, and for two or three years we shared the cottage at Clarehaven, till Victor moved to Michel Grove near Findon in Sussex, and I with him. Daultie, whose maiden name was Vestey, had been married to Maurice Kingscote, a fine horseman and huntsman and, like Geoff, something of a soldier of fortune. Her first husband was Phil Cripps, at one time a starter for the Jockey Club, of whom Geoff once remarked, "His address ought to be Number One Mappin Terrace." After years as a carefree bachelor with a series of girl friends, who tended to be other men's wives and good looking, and living on a permanent financial razor's edge, Geoff finally settled for marriage where money was. Daultie, as her family's name suggests, was rich and believed in living a life appropriate to her social status and sporting tastes, which fitted those of Geoff. She was typical of the smart women of the two decades before the second war. Tall and upright, with rather hard good looks, she was well dressed in typically English fashion and was fairly tough in character. Her prototype could have been seen in any *Tatler*, *Bystander* or *Sketch* of the period. I remember once going to the yard of Harold Field, the horse dealer at Chichester, with Daultie, Geoff and Victor Gilpin, to look at hunters. Harold and I were walking behind the others and he, with an expert eye for conformation and action, looking at Daultie, remarked to me, "The Major always liked a straight mover."

Geoff's new-found affluence and easier life had slowed him up somewhat and altered his outlook on life. He had become rather deaf, and where formerly he gave no thought to economy – he told me that he had only travelled in the Tube once in his life: "the chap never got a pull at it till we got to Arnos Grove, so I had to get a taxi in the end" – he now complained of such trivialities as the price of gin. But he had lost none of his wit and humour, nor was he overawed by his father-in-law, Lord Vestey. The latter was once running down racing and its followers to Geoff, saying it was a source of needless extravagance and a path to penury, when Geoff answered him: "It's like anything else, if you know your business you're all right, if you don't you go under. Take yourself: you're a butcher and know all about butchering, so you've made a go of it. If I tried butchering I'd probably go broke, but I do know something about racing and it's done me pretty well over the years." Jean and I used to dine with Geoff periodically. I always enjoyed his company and the house was run smoothly and efficiently by the butler, Cotten, a paragon of his profession who was once seen wading out into the stream where Geoff and Daultie were fishing, bearing a silver salver with two Dry Martinis on it. One evening when we arrived at Clatford Mill for dinner, Geoff came out to meet us and said: "We've got an artist staying with us. My father-in-law decided he would make us a present of a portrait of Daultie – it would have been much more to the point if he'd given us the money to buy a couple of yearlings instead – anyway, the fellow's been here about a fortnight and seems to like my port, as he shows no sign of moving. Either the light's in the wrong place, or it's too dull or too bright, so God knows when he'll be finished, and when he has we haven't got a lavatory big enough to put the picture in." Geoff had an original turn of phraseology. One of his favourite precepts was, "Never lay the odds, never travel entirely sober and never hunt south of the Thames," and in the old days at Clarehaven Cottage, when we split half a bottle of champagne – one of his side-lines was being an agent for a champagne company – he would raise his glass to the toast of, "Here's to our softening cocks and hardening arteries." Alas, Geoff died after a heart attack out shooting, in 1953. I have missed him greatly and often think of our happy days at Newmarket, his apt observations and practical advice. Nevertheless, old age would not have become him, nor would he have enjoyed it.

Herbie Pretyman, from whom we bought East Woodhay House, was formerly a regular officer in the Royal Navy. He was a close friend of 'Babe' (Lt-Colonel) Moseley, who had also begun his adult life at sea but suffered so badly from sea-sickness that he transferred to the Army, joining a cavalry regiment and becoming a successful amateur rider over fences. Babe was quite a bit older than I was and had given up race riding before the war ended, but continued to go well to hounds with the Beaufort, where we met again when Jean and I started hunting several years after I stopped riding in races. Together, Babe and Herbie owned a horse or two, notably Maisey Hampton, a good-looking chestnut gelding trained by Bill Payne senior, a first-class trainer under both Rules, whose horses were always turned out to perfection. The partners nearly brought off a coup in the Cambridgeshire, being foiled by heavy going, which Maisey Hampton disliked; as a result he was narrowly beaten into third place. They kindly gave me one or two rides on Maisey Hampton in amateur races on the flat, two of which he won. He was a lazy horse and needed hard riding, but I never had to hit him more than two or three times, keeping him going by swinging the whip at him and kicking him with my heels – an operation rendered virtually impossible by the modern fashion of flat race jockeys riding with ultra-short stirrup-leathers. The first race in which he carried me to victory was at Lewes, where he was so favourably handicapped as to be a certainty; he won easily but still had to be kept up to his work from the entrance to the straight. Our second success was at Leicester and was won narrowly after a long battle. When we turned for home our chances looked re-mote, but Maisey Hampton gradually made up ground and got up to win in the last few yards. Both these races were at one and a quarter miles and since he was always going best at the finish, I told Bill Payne that Maisey Hampton gave me the impression that he would get a mile and a half. He was tried over this distance – I think I rode him on this occasion – but proved that a mile and a quarter was his limit. When he retired from racing on the flat, Maisey Hampton won a number of point-to-points, his ability and relaxed jumping enabling him to stay the longer distances of this type of racing.

When serving a spell on the Staff at Western Command HQ in Chester during the war, I got to know Pat Dennis, a contemporary of Geoff Harbord. He had been a top-class amateur rider, winning the National Hunt 'Chase at Cheltenham, and later trained racehorses at his property, Stansty Park, outside Wrexham, where he owned a coal-mine, at that time, in the process of being nationalised. Pat was typical of a certain type of bright young man of the 1920s: immaculately turned out, fast-living – usually beyond their means – keen on field sports, generously hospitable, good company, and believers in having the best of every-thing, regardless of cost or the ability to pay in the foreseeable future. He served with the Brigade of Guards during the final months of the

1914–18 war, and after refusing the wish of his father to stay on as a regular soldier, in favour of a life on the Turf, he found himself cut off and, like a number of his contemporaries, living on his wits and resources, which he succeeded in doing. With the death of his father and the sale of the family coal-mine, his fortunes changed dramatically from uncertainty to affluence, which he exploited to the full. One of his trainers, the late Peter Hastings-Bass, observed to him, when Pat divulged the sum he proposed to put on one of his horses, "Steady on, you've inherited a coal-mine – not a gold mine." The sale of the coal-mine was being negotiated while I was at Western Command, Pat being represented by Hartley (now Lord) Shawcross, then a Socialist and later to leave the party for the cross benches. One weekend I was staying with Pat, Hartley Shawcross also being there. He was a pleasant, intelligent and highly civilised man, and seeing him, faultlessly attired, leaning back in an armchair after an excellent dinner, with a glass of Pat's fine brandy, I was amused at the incongruity of his politics with his lifestyle.

While I was at Western Command I got to know Pat well. He was in charge of entertainment – Kinema was, I think, the official title – and his office was near to that of the Military Secretary, in which I held a minor position. We met daily and often I spent a weekend at Stansty with him and his attractive wife, Babe, who also worked in the Command. I had bought a brood mare earlier during the ear and started breeding in a small way, but had no stud of my own; so when, shortly after the war, Pat offered to keep them at Stansty, where he had a horse or two of his own, we decided to go into partnership, breeding yearlings for sale and keeping the odd filly in training. Later he moved for a spell to Ireland, buying the Greenmount Stud in Co. Limerick and hunting with the local hounds. We continued our partnership with the bloodstock and bred a pretty good horse, which was bought as a yearling for 2000 guineas by Sir Victor Sassoon and named by him Stokes. The choice of this name was not without humour: the colt was by Sir Victor's own stallion, Mieuxce, out of Brazen Molly. The girlfriend of Sir Victor's brother-in-law, Derrick Fitzgerald, was Molly Stokes. Stokes was trained by Norman Bertie, whose stable was owned and managed by Jack Clayton, who later took out a trainer's licence himself. The policy of the stable was to under-train rather than over-train horses, which did not suit Stokes, a fine-looking colt but big, powerful and obstreperous. As a result Stokes was never really fit, but despite this disadvantage he won the Newmarket Spring two-year-old Stakes and Windsor Castle Stakes at Royal Ascot; and ran second in The Two Thousand Guineas and the Derby

Trial Stakes at Lingfield, ending his days at stud in Australia. Jean and I stayed with Pat several times and always enjoyed these visits, but he never really settled in Ireland where the happy-go-lucky nature of life did not fit in with his meticulous principles of domestic and estate management. He could not get accustomed to people failing to keep appointments for meals, but turning up uninvited, perhaps still in their hunting clothes, and servants laying the table improperly, and such actions as guests burning holes with cigarettes in new carpets because it made the house look as if it was lived in. So he moved back to England, settling in Gloucestershire.

Amongst the other winners Pat and I bred was a filly destined to have a stupendous influence in Australia and beyond. This was a beautiful little bay called Oceana, by The Two Thousand Guineas winner Colombo (by Manna-Lady Nairne, by Chaucer) out of the first mare I ever owned, Orama (by Diophon-Cantelupe, by Amadis). We put Oceana in training ourselves with Marcus Marsh at Egerton House, Newmarket, whence she won a maiden two-year-old race at Haydock, ridden by the good Australian jockey Edgar Britt. Marcus Marsh – son of the Royal trainer Dick Marsh responsible for the Royal classic winners Persimmon, Minoru and Diamond Jubilee – had trained the pre-war Derby and St. Leger winner, Windsor Lad (by Blandford-Resplendent, by By George!) whom Charlie Smirke, rider of Windsor Lad as a three and four-year-old, rated better than the unbeaten Bahram (by Blandford-Friar's Daughter, by Friar Marcus), partnered by Smirke in The St. Leger. Marcus had been a rear gunner in the RAF during the war, being shot down and taken prisoner. When he started training again after the war he soon acquired a stable of useful horses, a number of owners being sympathetic to him, owing to his war record, among them Pat, who gave him all the equipment and clothing that he had from his own training days. Thus Pat was not unnaturally rather hurt when the following season, on being sent the Aga Khan's horses on the retirement of Frank Butters, Marsh asked Pat and me to take our horses away on the pretext that Pat, who liked a bet but never touted a trainer about other owners' horses, would be better suited to a betting stable. Moreover, Marsh accepted to train two expensive yearlings for a new owner, the Duke of Devonshire. Two friends from pre-war days, theirs at Cambridge and mine at Newmarket, Nicky Morriss, who was at Wellington with me, and Dan Ranfurly (the Earl of Ranfurly, who died in 1987), owned a filly in partnership, My Poppet, trained by Marcus Marsh. My Poppet was bred at the Banstead Manor Stud started by Nicky's father Harry, who won The Derby with Manna. The stud went downhill till Nicky took it over from his mother and put it on a successful footing; he also set up the White Lodge Stud, which did so well for the Moller brothers and was sold to Sheikh Mohammed after the brothers' death. Dan and I, for a season before the war, both kept a horse at livery with Terence Hone in the Fitzwilliam country and opposed each other in point-to-points at Cottenham. A prisoner of war in Italy, Dan afterwards became Governor and C-in-C of the Bahamas, a member of the Jockey Club and part-owner of several useful horses on the flat. My Poppet was in a race at Yarmouth together with a stable companion owned by the Aga Khan and fancied most of the two by Marsh. However the partners thought differently, believing that My Poppet had been ridden the wrong way when beaten in her previous race. While Marsh was attending to the Aga's horse, ridden by the top jockey, Doug Smith, they gave their own instructions to My Poppet's rider, an apprentice, and sent him out while Marsh was still busy with his more favoured runner. The outcome was that My Poppet won and the Aga's horse was unplaced. Marsh was furious and declined to enter the winner's enclosure to greet the victorious My Poppet. In the long run the changes in his stable did Marsh no good. Though he trained Tulyar (by Tehran-Neocracy, by Nearco) to win The Derby, St. Leger, King George VI and the Queen Elizabeth Stakes and the Eclipse, the Aga removed his horses to France after a couple of seasons, giving as a reason that racing there was more lucrative. He never forgave Marsh for taking Tulyar out of The Two Thousand Guineas which, on form through King's Bench, arguably Tulyar could have won. The following season the Aga allowed Marsh to spend a great deal of money on yearlings, all of which proved more or less useless. Added to this Marsh did not find favour with Prince Aly Khan, who liked a bet and for which purpose Marsh seemed unable to provide winners. From then on he seemed to lose heart in the business, his stable dwindled and he retired into obscurity. It is rather a sad story, as Marcus Marsh was a fine stableman, had learnt the game thoroughly under his father and his uncle Fred Darling, and proved he could train classic winners. He gave me several winning rides in amateur races, a couple on a grand horse by Blue Peter called Boy Blue, who belonged to Windsor Lad's first owner, the Maharaja of Rajpipla, who later sold Windsor Lad to Martin Benson, after his failure in the Eclipse as a three-year-old. The one to come out best from the incident was Benson, who got the horse cheaper because he lost.

When Pat and I had to leave Marcus Marsh, Oceana was a three-year-

Philadelphe II (J.H.) winning easily at Windsor.

East Woodhay House where Brigadier Gerard was reared.

Jean and Andrew (left) with J.H. and Ian at East Woodhay House.

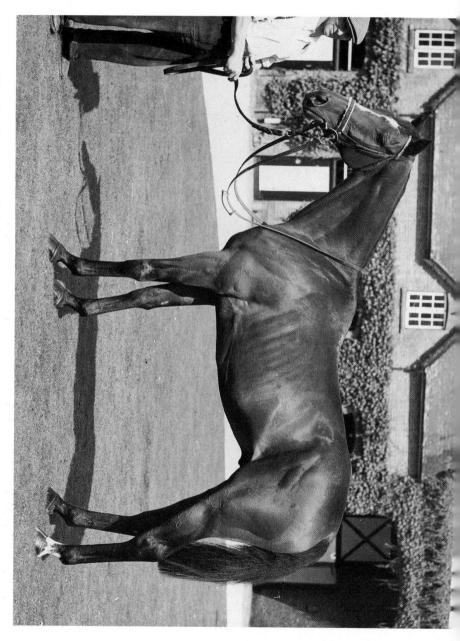

Tickled Pink, winner of all 6 races in which he carried J.H., in the stableyard at Manton.

old and we sent her to Evan Williams at Kingsclere, which was convenient, being close to East Woodhay House. Evan and Gill Williams were old friends of Jean and mine from pre-war days. Evan, a first-class rider over fences who won the Grand National on Royal Mail, used to have the same racecourse valet as I, Charlie Stalker, and rode for Ivor Anthony, one of the outstanding trainers of jumpers in modern times. Referring to another trainer, a friend once remarked to me: "He was a bad trainer, but he was fun to train with"; and since few racehorses pay their way it is as well to have some fun out of them. If they are any good they will probably win something, whoever trains them, and while a top trainer will do better than an average one, the clients of such establishments may find themselves so distanced from the trainer, their horses and the running plans that they might as well have their money in stocks and shares. With Evan Williams, things were different: the whole business was always fun, clients could share in the stable bets, see their horses when they wanted and enjoy the hospitality offered by Evan and his wife. For me there was the added enjoyment of riding work regularly, sometimes on our own horses, sometimes on others in the stable. One morning I had the privilege of riding Supreme Court, unbeaten as a three-year-old and winner of the first running of the King George VI and Queen Elizabeth Stakes, that year known as the Festival of Britain Stakes. When I rode him, Supreme Court was a backward two-year-old, whose merit was unknown. He was a big, fine horse and a nice mover, but changed his legs halfway up the canter, which is sometimes a sign of immaturity. By Precipitation, Supreme Court was out of Forecourt, by Fair Trial out of Overture, the last-named a beautiful filly trained by Victor Gilpin when I was assistant to him. Overture was by Dastur out of Overmantle, by Apron out of Arabella, a granddaughter of Pretty Polly. Supreme Court was bred by the late Thomas Lilley and raced in the name of his wife Vera, Mrs. Hue-Williams, who were neighbours of ours, living at Woolton House. Evan was not one of their usual trainers, Noel Murless and Marcus Marsh, but the latter two turned down the offer to train Supreme Court, because he had a twisted foreleg, so the Lilleys approached Evan, as he was nearby at Kingsclere, who accepted him. It was a happy choice, since Supreme Court was a delicate horse, needed little work and though courageous and well-behaved on the racecourse, was sometimes a bit of a handful at home. I remember seeing him standing up on his hind legs one morning. Evan understood the horse, was patient with him and trained him to perfection, giving him only the lightest of preparations. He told me that the only time Supreme

73

Court had anything like a serious pre-race gallop, he did not win as impressively as usual and this was never repeated. Supreme Court retired at the end of his three-year-old season to his owners' stud. He was a fairly successful sire, a number of his stock inheriting his delicate constitution, but his name crops up in the pedigree of a good winner every now and then.

The stable jockey was Charlie Elliott, who used to ride work twice a week. He lived in London but despite the distance from Kingsclere he was never late for first lot. Elliott was both a first-class jockey and work-rider, qualities by no means always reciprocal; for instance, Vincent O'Brien once pronounced Lester Piggott a brilliant race-rider but not a good work rider, because he always tried to find out too much about the horse he was on. When still an apprentice, Charlie Elliott was equal leading jockey with the great Steve Donoghue and first jockey to Jack Jarvis. He was rather wild as a young man, his trouble being gambling, as a result of which he departed to France where, until the war, he rode for Marcel Boussac, and had great success. At the time of which I write, Elliott was mature and settled in England. One of the best races he ever rode was on Supreme Court in the Festival of Britain Stakes. In this race, most of the jockeys set off at a furious pace, except Elliott and Piggott (on Zucchero), and most horses were spent by the end, enabling Elliott and Piggott to finish first and second. The Derby winner Arctic Prince, who was more judiciously ridden by Charlie Spares, his jockey at Epsom, broke down in the race when going well, but might not have beaten Supreme Court in any case.

Charlie was most entertaining when we foregathered at breakfast after work and he talked about his racing experiences. He told of Lord Rosebery, the Prime Minister, who had won The Derby three times with Ladas, Sir Visto and Cicero, but had never won a 'Cup'. In the Jockey Club Cup at Newmarket in 1924 the occasion to achieve this seemed to have arrived. There were three runners, Rosebery's filly, The One Thousand Guineas winner Plack ridden by Charlie Smirke, because Elliott could not do the weight of 7st. 9lbs – Smirke had not put on weight at this stage of his career – Elliott on Eastern Monarch, and Ceylonese with Michael Beary up. Plack was two to one on, there appeared to be no danger and the three riders agreed that Plack would be given as easy a task as possible. Unfortunately Plack was in an unco-operative mood and it took every effort on the part of Smirke to get her first past the post, and of the other two to ensure that this was achieved. After the race, Lord Rosebery observed: "I always wanted to win a Cup –

but not that way." Charlie Elliott was extremely lucid on race riding, and his advice was a great help to me in my efforts. After he retired he trained for a short time, but this was not his metier. He had little success, retired and, unfortunately, died in 1979 in poor circumstances, due it is feared to betting.

For a time I had a small share in the stable bets: it was an added interest, but we ran into a spell of bad luck, which was rather too much for my nerves, though we got out of trouble on a filly called Batta who, despite her temperamentally volatile breeding, by Nasrullah out of a mare by Bois Roussel, was stout and genuine. Running on gallantly, Batta just got up to win a handicap at Hurst Park, ridden by Manny Mercer.

We were lucky in finding three excellent schools locally, to which our two boys went at different stages: an infant class run by Miss New and held at Stargroves, then the home of Sir Frederick and Lady Carden; Gorselands, a pre-prep school, in Newbury; and Horris Hill, which was near East Woodhay, under the direction of the Stows, many of whose people went on to Winchester. This grounding helped them to scholarships at Winchester and Cambridge. We asked Andrew whether many boys at Horris Hill were homesick. He replied: "Only the ones who have dogs!" Any genetic influence for the boys' academic success is due to Jean rather than to me, since she has the better brain, while my academic ceiling was four credits in the School Certificate, in English, History, French and German, and the need for private tuition to get me through the paper in mathematics – the young man who coached me was morally rewarded by ending up a bishop. An interesting contrast in pre-war and modern attitudes in schools showed itself in a remark of our elder son Ian, who was captain of the Colts cricket XI at Winchester. When I suggested that he would probably be in the 1st XI the following year, he answered: "No, it would interfere with my work too much," a philosophy inconceivable in my time at Wellington.

The literary world is far removed from that of the Turf, but about then we got to know two eminent figures in the former milieu, Anthony Powell, whom with his wife Violet we met staying with the d'Avigdor-Goldsmids at Somerhill, and John and Penelope Betjeman, who lived at Wantage and were mutual friends with Desmond and Molly Baring. Anthony Powell and John Betjeman had in common complete unpretentiousness, commendable modesty about their work, and being excellent company. Anthony and I had a mutual acquaintance in a tedious

75

colonel, with whom he served during the war and introduced into one of his books, and whose wife had a horse trained by Victor Gilpin when I was his assistant before the war. John Betjeman was exactly as he has been described in print and depicted on television. He was amused to learn that I knew of the prep-school at which he taught for a short time, when I lived at Gerrards Cross as a boy. Describing his unsuitability for the task, he related that when he enquired whether a boy had gone to the lavatory after breakfast, this being one of his duties, he was liable to be answered: "Have you, sir?" Jean and I liked both John and Penelope, but they could not have been more different. John appreciated home comforts, good wine and food; Penelope disapproved of drink – on one occasion she emptied some of John's best claret into the fishpond – and was impervious to discomfort: "If I'm cold I just put on another pair of combinations." She was a bold rider to hounds and I can recall her attacking a fearsome looking obstacle which, improbably, included an iron bedstead, out with the Old Berks, on a horse which she had bought at Reading market for £50. For convenience sake she built a stable a few yards from the kitchen window, regardless of the environmental effect. As opposed to John, who enjoyed acquiring odd, useless pieces of information, such as the lyrics and melodies of school songs, Penelope was entirely practical. One of the few characteristics they had in common was that each was religious. In view of John's choice of subjects for his poems and his general tastes, I was astonished when, one day, we were lunching with the Betjemans, he drew me into his study, took down a book by 'The Druid', who wrote on hunting, racing and country life and read out a passage, exclaiming "Great stuff, isn't it?"

One of our neighbours whom we saw quite often was Porchey, the late 6th Earl of Carnarvon who died in 1987. Short in stature, squarely built and given to a slightly flamboyant taste in dress, he resembled something between a bookmaker and a stage comedian; indeed his character embraced a little of each. Good company, he was amusing, mannerless, a gourmet and spoke good French; he was kind, unscrupulous, often mean, sometimes generous and was fond of children; a good judge of racing, paradoxically he tended to be foolish in the management of his own horses, though capable of giving others sound advice about theirs; he was a fine shot, a keen amateur rider on the flat – "You don't want to ride jumping, people get paid for that," he advised his son, Henry now 7th Earl of Carnarvon and rode a number of winners, though far from a polished performer – unkind racegoers termed him 'the flying pig'; ardent in the pursuit of ladies' favours, he was much liked by his employees who served him loyally, especially his impeccable butler, Robert. We often met dining at Highclere Castle, his home, or at East Woodhay House, and on the racecourse. An enthusiastic card player, he once telephoned to ask us to dinner at short notice, adding that he had an American couple staying with him, and that with Jean, also a good card player, they could make up a four at bridge. I, not being a bridge player, could read the magazines or go home after dinner. From Jean I gathered that when they sat down to play, Porchey said to his house guests: "I expect you know each other's play, so you can play together and I'll partner Jean." To Jean's surprise, he named the house stakes as astronomically higher than usual, and when she observed that they were too much for her, told her, "That's all right, I'll carry you for the surplus." Before a hand had been played Jean realised that not only were the Americans poor players, but they barely understood the game, the outcome being that they had an extremely expensive evening, capped by being presented with a photograph of their host in full regalia of a Peer of the Realm, together with a bill for £25. He adopted the latter ruse with his two autobiographies, telling the victims that he was sending them a signed copy, which arrived with the bill inside. Speaking to Porchey on the telephone the next day, Jean remonstrated with him for fleecing his guests, to which he replied: "Don't worry, they've got plenty of money." Yet had a friend in financial trouble approached Porchey, I am certain he would have come to the rescue. Indeed, Robin Scully, now an eminent racehorse owner and breeder in the USA and Europe, told me that from his schooldays he had received nothing but kindness and helpful advice from Porchey.

Porchey's racing was always hampered by his policy of "better sell and regret than keep and regret". As a result he sold the subsequent Derby winner Blenheim as a yearling, the latter's half brother King Salmon as a two-year-old before he ran second in The Two Thousand Guineas and Derby and won the Eclipse, and Blenheim's full brother His Grace, for less than the horse won in prize money. For a time Porchey was a Steward at Salisbury, when he was rumoured to be not above betting on races in which he was officiating. Once I'm pretty sure he backed a horse ridden by me, having quizzed me about the horse beforehand, observing "You'll be pretty unpopular if you don't win." There was a close finish in which my horse got the verdict, the second lodging an objection for interference. Comparing our respective questioning in the Stewards' Room by Porchey, Bobby Petre, who rode the second, and I were in no doubt as to whose side he was on. The objection was overruled. Once I rode a horse for him in a race advertised at one-and-a-quarter miles but later changed to one-and-a-half-miles, a distance beyond the horse's best. However in the change Porchey saw an opportunity to benefit himself. Owing to my run of luck in amateur races the horse was an automatic favourite, so his owner made arrangements to lay it, stressing that he did not want the horse knocked about. While we were standing in the paddock before the race, his emissary dashed up to Porchey saying that he had succeeded in laying the horse to lose the required amount. Whereupon Porchey hissed at him: "Shut up you stupid fool, can't you see Lord Sefton – a Steward of the Jockey Club – is standing five yards away?" The horse failed to stay and finished second. I have never ridden for an owner so pleased at being beaten. At one time he had horses with Fred Darling, and out on the downs watching work one day he had the temerity to wave the lads on to go faster, so that he could find out the form for future use. Fred, a martinet in anything regarding his horse, exploded with fury and banished him from the stable. Porchey ceased to be a steward before I finished race riding. Unsurprisingly, he was never elected to the Jockey Club and was far from pleased when his son Henry was. We also saw a good deal of Henry and had a pleasant holiday with him one year in St. Moritz. A keen owner-breeder, Henry is a good judge of a yearling, one of his purchases being Tamerlane, with whom he later was unlucky not to win The Two Thousand, owing to Breasley's unfamiliarity with the course. As Chairman of Newbury race-course, Henry took a major part in the rebuilding of the stands, completed in 1992. He also devised the Newbury Sales Super Sprint Trophy for 2-year-olds, worth nearly £60,000 to the winner, his filly Lyric Fantasy taking the first running of the race, in 1992.

For a good many years Henry has managed The Queens' racehorses.

Another close neighbour was Dick Dawson, the Aga Khan's first trainer, then retired, and with his full, white moustache and pince-nez, looking more like an academic than one of his profession. Though old and in poor health, his mind was clear and sharp, and he liked to talk of the Turf, past and present. The best horse he ever trained, he said, was Mumtaz Mahal, allowing that she was a pure sprinter; his two Derby winners, Blenheim and Trigo, he rated inferior to her. Of Trigo he said that The Derby took so much out of him that for a long time afterwards he would not have won a 'seller'. In consequence Trigo did not race again until winning The St. Leger by a short head from the next year's Ascot Gold Cup winner, Bosworth. Trigo's only other race was the Irish St Leger, also won by a short head, but the conditions of the race required him to give the second, Visellus, 12lbs. Despite being by the outstanding classic sire, Blandford, whom Dick Dawson bred and owned, Trigo was a failure at stud, probably due to the somewhat plebeian breeding of his dam. There was an argument as to who should ride Trigo in The St. Leger. The stable jockey, Michael Beary, chose to ride Le Voleur in The Derby, Joe Marshall having the mount on Trigo. Seemingly, the stable jockey should automatically have ridden Trigo, but the matter was put to the Jockey Club for decision, who came down in favour of Beary. It may have been that Dick Dawson would have preferred Marshall, as he told me that he disliked Beary as a jockey because he was too free and severe with the whip. That Beary became the stable jockey was, I believe through the influence of the Aga Khan and not by Dawson's choice.

Dick Dawson worked his horses hard, but was a successful trainer, being one of the few to have prepared a winner of the Grand National, Drogheda, and a Derby winner. In assessing a yearling, he used to say: "I can't abide a perfect horse", a precept borne out when, against Dawson's advice, the Aga Khan insisted on buying an expensive, faultless individual, immaculately bred, which proved useless.

Colonel Fred Cripps, a younger brother of Sir Stafford Cripps, an austere, dedicated and eminent Labour politician and statesman, whose various important posts included Ambassador to Russia in 1940. The brothers were far removed in character, politics and lifestyle, despite which they got on well. Fred once told me of a meeting with Dick Dawson in Dover Street: "He asked me to accompany him on his way to meet a prospective owner, outside the Bath Club in Dover Street. 'Why outside the Bath Club?' I said. 'Oh, this is the sort of man you wouldn't take into a decent pub,' he answered. "It wasn't till after I married that I realised he had been referring to my future father-in-law," Fred added.

While we lived far from Newmarket, where I spent the first five years of my racing life from 1931 to 1936, we often stayed there, as I attended all the chief race meetings on the two courses. For the Craven Meeting we usually went to Cicely Lambton at Mesnil Warren, of which I had many happy memories before the war, when George Lambton was alive and the two younger children, Teddy and his sister Billie, were living at home. Teddy had been a good amateur rider on the flat, but was tall and had a problem with his weight, so after the war took out a trainer's licence. He had a flair for training and a way with horses, sending out many winners, among them Langton Abbot, with whom he brought off a coup in the Lincolnshire Handicap, a race he also won with Mighty

Gurkha, as well as being responsible for that good sprinter Compensation. His financial downfall came as a result of complete ignorance of and disregard for business procedure, added to the odd betting disaster and an inherent philosophy that only the best was good enough whether affordable or not. Happily the family fortunes turned to enable him to end his days in comfort and affluence. Teddy had a good brain and wrote well, but except for one or two articles in The British Racehorse, did not exploit this talent, was a delightful companion and a generous host; he and his second wife Pauline made Mesnil Warren a happy and comfortable home, the hospitality of which their many friends enjoyed. Though Teddy's mother Cicely Lambton had fine qualities, she was besotted with Teddy and ruined him through her devotion, taking him away from Eton early for no other reason than that she wanted him at home, and letting him loose on the fast-living, hard-drinking life of the racing element of Newmarket in the 1930s, at an early age. I can remember Charlie Waugh, the trainer next door to Clarehaven, where I worked, saying to me: "The Lambtons are ruining that boy keeping him at home; they ought to send him away to a strict trainer like Mr. Persse." Alas, this did not happen and the promise of an outstanding career was never properly fulfilled. Cicely Lambton herself never seemed to change over the years. A woman of courage, fortitude and physical toughness, she came from an academic background, and while she was inclined to rap on the dinner table and rebuke a guest for leading the conversation away from racing, she was as likely to pour scorn on any expression of literary ignorance. Apart from having to cope with the various troubles of Teddy's youth, she had to face the death of her eldest son, John, who was killed flying during the war, and that of her younger daughter, Billie, in a point-to-point some years later. Her eldest daughter, Nancy, was a Persian scholar of repute, and disappeared into the world of academe, seldom emerging. Considerably younger than her husband and a beauty in her youth, Cicely was not without her admirers and had firm ideas on social mores: "Adultery is no reason for divorce", she once announced in the course of conversation. A story, possibly apocryphal, used to be told in the higher echelons of pre-war Newmarket society that, once, George Lambton had set off to go racing and found he had forgotten his race glasses, so returned to fetch them. Meanwhile, Cicely was dallying on the drawing room sofa with an admirer and, on hearing George enter the hall, called out, with great presence of mind: "Don't come into the drawing room, George, the canary's out of its cage." To the last, Cicely remained an active racegoer and keen punter; and it was a great joy to her declining years to see Teddy happily married to Pauline and to be able to enjoy the racing successes of their home-bred horses, which Teddy managed.

After the war and until I gave up race riding, I rode a great deal for Sam Armstrong in amateur races on the flat and used to ride out for him regularly whenever I stayed at Newmarket. He was a top-class trainer and in the heyday of his chief patron, the Maharajah of Baroda, had some beautiful horses, a number of which I was lucky enough to ride and to see work. In 1947, Sam Armstrong was sent to train the best horse he ever had in his stable, My Babu. By Djebel out of Perfume II, by Badruddin, My Babu was bred in France by Peter Beatty, who won The Derby with Bois Roussel. He was bought privately by the Baroda, unseen by Sam. I was riding out with Sam shortly after the colt arrived at Warren Place. "Come and have a look at what the Baroda's just bought", he said. My Babu, who at that time bore the name of Lerins, was not an imposing yearling. He was small, rather rough in his coat and had perceptibly bent hind legs – a legacy from his paternal grandsire, Tourbillon – with more than the suspicion of a curb on one of them. Moreover he was already broken and had been tried over three furlongs in France, on the outcome of which the purchase had been made and the price, reputedly substantial, agreed. The Baroda must be classed as a lucky owner, for My Babu turned out to be another Sayajirao, but better. Under Sam's care he improved out of all recognition, growing and developing into a most attractive two-year-old, typical of his sire, Djebel. He was full of quality, a lovely, easy mover and like all Sam's horses always looked in beautiful condition.

At that time Edgar Britt, the Australian jockey, was riding for Sam and having great success. Horses went well for him and he never knocked them about. Sam hated to see horses punished, on the theory that the more enjoyable racing could be made for them the better they would run. Whenever I rode for Sam I only went for the whip as a last resort, and then used it sparingly.

My Babu began his racing career as Lerins, his name being changed between his two-year-old and three-year-old seasons, the choice of My Babu being on account of this being the nickname of the Baroda's son. The superstition held by some racing people that it is unlucky to change a horse's name has little foundation. My Babu first appeared in the Hyde Park Stakes at Epsom, in which he finished fourth to Delirium (Panorama-Passed Out, by Solario), a handsome chestnut colt trained by Jack Leach. Sam had a penchant for Epsom, and he always left a bit to work on with his two-year-olds first time out, so My Babu's debut was propitious. Promise was fulfilled when he proceeded to win his remaining five races, which included the Woodcote Stakes at Epsom, the Champagne Stakes at Doncaster and dead-heating with Delirium for the New Stakes at Ascot.

Sam Armstrong, who died in December 1983, was a trainer of outstanding ability. I first got to know him through riding a flat race winner called Domaha (Vatout-Proserpine II, by Eugene de Savoie) for him in 1937; the horse had recently been imported from France, was beaten two heads in the Cambridgeshire the following season and became a good sire of jumpers. During the years I rode for him I got to know Sam well and to like him. Though a disciplinarian, he looked after his lads conscientiously and took much trouble in getting rides for his apprentices. Among the successful jockeys he produced are Willie Carson, Wally Swinburn, Willie Snaith, Josh Gifford and Paul Tulk. A master stableman, Sam Armstrong turned his horses out immaculately and kept his yard impeccably. When you rode for him he imbued confidence: "Good luck, win if you can but it won't be the end of the world if you don't," he would say as he led the horse out on to the course, which he always did himself; and he never grumbled at defeat. Most of the horses Sam put me on won; they were carefully placed and as often as not had a good bit in hand. Sam was extremely particular in buying yearlings, or for that matter any horse. He bought a number of horses in training in France, and he would never consider one that was not a good individual. Thus when training and buying for the Maharajah of Baroda he acquired a magnificent string appropriately stabled in the fine Warren Place establishment. Later, when he moved to St. Gatien – named after the horse who dead-heated with Harvester for The Derby of 1884 – after the Baroda's horses left, Sam maintained the same high standards of efficiency and selectivity. Traditionally the box doors at St. Gatien were painted orange, the metal work silver, which Sam retained, adding various improvements to the property. He was an early riser and when I arrived to ride out at 6.45 in the morning he would be going round the yard or sitting at the typewriter in the office, which looked out on to the stables. He never missed a detail and if a horse came out with an item of tack out of place he was on to it in a flash. The atmosphere of the yard was one of well-ordered bustle, reflected in Sam's speech and action.

Edgar Britt and Charlie Smirke were riding for the stable at that time, which did not make life too easy for Sam as they disliked each other strongly. Smirke's engagement for the Baroda's horses was due, I believe, to the influence of the Maharanee, who was also said to have caused the horses to be removed later, first to Tommy Carey and then to Peter Nelson. I did not meet the Maharanee, but several times encountered the Baroda, whom I found a jovial, agreeable character of medium height and a shade portly. Though respecting Smirke's ability, Sam preferred Britt and, when My Babu won The Two Thousand, Sam got the photographer to make him a print of My Babu's posed photograph showing Britt in the saddle. Sam left no stone unturned in acquiring owners and had no scruples in luring them away from other trainers, on the principle that it was a tough game and a case of each man for himself. In spite of this he was liked among his colleagues, as he had great kindness and would always help anyone if he could. He treated his owners with a diplomacy which sometimes backfired, when his encouraging reports of horses' running proved to have been over-gilded: "ran a nice race" might turn out to be an interpretation for the horse having finished 24th of 25 runners. "Never finish last if you can help it" was one of Sam's injunctions to riders, on the principle that though the form book invariably indicated the horse to finish last, no mention was made of the intervening places after the first half-dozen.

The segregation of the different classifications of owners, who were being entertained at St. Gatien after going round stables during race week always intrigued me. In one room were the top echelon, Jockey Club Members, titled owners and tycoons; in the next business-men, small owner-breeders and commercial breeders; in the third coloured owners. All the while Sam and Maureen his wife would be darting from one room to the other plying each faction with drinks, Sam endeavouring to give every owner the impression that he and his horses were the most important in the stable. Sam's mind was always on the job. Even on Christmas Day he seldom got as far as the Christmas pudding before jumping up and dashing to his office to tap out letters to his owners. He was a most prolific letter-writer and I never remember a Christmas without a letter or Christmas card from him and, when I was riding for him, a goose.

When, after developing heart trouble, Sam retired and handed over the stable to his son Robert, he could not bear the inactivity and was never happier than when standing in for Robert in the latter's absence. Sam's house, opposite the entrance to the Sale Paddocks, in the Avenue, was well-placed for visitors and, like many of his old friends, I always looked in to see him when at Newmarket. After the sad mental breakdown of his wife, Sam was very lonely and greatly appreciated people coming to see him. To the end he was alert and entertaining. I spoke to Sam on the telephone the day before he died and found him cheerful but not well: "I've had a touch of angina; I was supposed to be going to lunch with Noel and Gwen Murless, but don't feel up to it." The next day Keith Piggott, father of Sam's son-in-law Lester, called in to see Sam and found him dead in his chair.

6

A TIME OF CLASS AND CONSISTENCY

The 1947 season was one of good two-year-olds. At Beckhampton, Fred Darling trained a high-class colt belonging to Lt. Colonel Giles Loder, called The Cobbler (Windsor Slipper-Overture, by Dastur), a descendant of the famous Pretty Polly, who was bred and owned by Giles Loder's uncle, Eustace. The Cobbler was unbeaten in his five races that year, these including the Coventry Stakes at Ascot, the National Breeders' Stakes at Sandown in which he beat Delirium a length at level weights, and the Middle Park Stakes by a head from Birthday Greetings (Blue Peter-Clarapple, by Apple Sammy), a big, powerful chestnut colt belonging to Miss Dorothy Paget and trained by Henri Jelliss. Birthday Greetings won the Richmond Stakes at Goodwood and the Gainsborough Stakes at Hurst Park, but did not stay beyond six or seven furlongs.

Yet another good colt of that year was Black Tarquin (Rhodes Scholar-Vagrancy, by Sir Gallahad III), bred in the USA by his owner, Mr William Woodward, and trained by Cecil (later Sir Cecil) Boyd-Rochfort. He was a big, strongly-made black colt, well put together with great heart room and a straight hind leg, but a bad walker, having an unusually short stride for his size. Black Tarquin did not give the impression of being a fast two-year-old, yet he won, in four starts, the Royal Lodge Stakes (then a five furlong race) and the Gimcrack Stakes beating by a head Birthday Greetings, to whom he had failed by two lengths to give 9lbs in the Richmond Stakes at Goodwood. Black Tarquin was a failure at stud, apart from siring some useful jumpers. The Cobbler was a length in front of Delirium on their running at Sandown. Birthday Greetings ran The

Cobbler to a head in the Middle Park Stakes; while Black Tarquin beat Birthday Greetings by a head in the Gimcrack.

With justification, the senior handicapper, Geoffrey Freer, could have come up with several permutations. His rating in the Free Handicap was as follows:

My Babu	9.7
The Cobbler	9.5
Black Tarquin	9.5
Birthday Greetings	9.4
Delirium	9.3

In making this handicap Freer was apparently bearing in mind that the Free Handicap is run over seven furlongs and that the horses assessed would then be three-year-olds. Thus he placed My Babu 4 lbs above Delirium (who also won the Prix Morny at Deauville), though they had dead-heated at level weights, and 2lbs in front of The Cobbler, who had beaten Delirium a length on equal terms. Time was to prove him right.

Before the 1948 season the Baroda had replaced Edgar Britt by Charlie Smirke as his jockey, a change not approved by Sam, who got on well with Britt but not with Smirke, though admitting the latter's ability. Thus it was Smirke who was in the saddle when My Babu made his first appearance as a three-year-old, in the Craven Stakes over the Rowley Mile at Newmarket, which he won by a comfortable half-length from Jim Joel's Pride of India, by Colombo. The Two Thousand Guineas of 1948 resulted in a desperate struggle between My Babu and The Cobbler, who was ridden by Gordon Richards and now trained by Noel Murless, Fred Darling having retired. My Babu won by a head from The Cobbler, Pride of India was third, four lengths back, and Birthday Greetings fourth. My Babu's next race was The Derby. Before the day he suffered a mishap which may have cost him the race. In his preparation he sustained a slight cut just above one of his hooves and as a precaution was given an anti-tetanus injection. Unfortunately he suffered a reaction, a swelling developed in his chest, where the injection was made, he went off colour and was stopped in his work. So he came to Epsom under a cloud, though remaining favourite at 4–1. Sam was worried that he had not been able to give My Babu a thorough preparation. In the race My Babu was not helped by being bumped and carried wide at Tattenham Corner, by Black Tarquin. He got to within a length of Royal Drake, who was making the running, but then weakened, finishing fourth behind My Love, Royal Drake and Noor. My Babu was not a true mile-and-a-half horse, so might not have won anyway, but he had more speed than the three who beat him and save for his misfortunes could possibly have just lasted home. My Babu did not regain his form that season; however, he returned as a four-year-old to win the Victoria Cup under 9st. 7lbs by three lengths from Pride of India (8st. 9lbs) and two minor races from four starts. His single defeat that season was by his old rival Delirium who, receiving 2lbs, beat him a head in the Crawfurd Handicap over six furlongs at Newmarket. It is remarkable how well the form of this vintage worked out over three seasons.

The Cobbler, who failed to stay in The Derby, continued to shine over sprint distances, his victories including the Wokingham Handicap at Royal Ascot with 9st. 4lbs. At the time, as before the war, the important handicaps still carried much prestige and attracted horses of classic merit. Prize money in France was not high enough to draw more than the odd English-trained runner, with the result that good horses had to run for what was going in England, the important handicaps providing some of the most attractive lures. It certainly made racing more interesting than when the best horses have the inducement to avoid each other through valuable, alternative engagements. Black Tarquin, who disappointed his stable badly in The Derby, perhaps because Epsom did not suit him, came back to his best when he won the St. James's Palace Stakes and The St. Leger.

Before The St. Leger, the final classic of the season, took place a new contender appeared on the scene. This was Alycidon, an imposing, rangy, truly made and handsome chestnut colt owned by Lord Derby, being home bred, and trained by Walter Earl. By Donatello II out of Aurora, by Hyperion out of Rose Red, by Swynford, he had a flawless staying pedigree. His third dam Marchetta (Marco-Hettie Sorrel) was the fourth dam of My Babu. Too big and backward to be exploited as a two-year-old, Alycidon ran twice unplaced that year. At three he soon made his presence felt by winning the Thirsk Classic Trial over a mile. After running third in the Chester Vase, giving weight to the winner, Valognes, and to the second, Wainwright, he won the Royal Standard Stakes at Manchester, ten furlongs. The race in which Alycidon showed that he was of genuine classic merit was the Princess of Wales' Stakes at Newmarket, one-and-a-half miles. In this event he beat the previous year's St. Leger winner, Sayajiraro, by two lengths on 4lbs worse terms than weight for age. Moreover, on his pedigree, Alycidon was entitled to be better suited to the extra distance of The St. Leger, than to the one-and-a-half miles of the Newmarket race.

Black Tarquin's pedigree did not indicate so much stamina as that of Alycidon. His sire, Rhodes Scholar (Pharos-Book Law, by Buchan), failed to win beyond the ten furlongs of the Eclipse Stakes, his other two victories, the St. James's Palace Stakes and the Ribblesdale Stakes (now one-and-a-half miles, for fillies) being at a mile. Vagrancy, dam of Black Tarquin, was by Sir Gallahad III out of Valkyr, by Man o'War out of Princess Palatine, by Prince Palatine; thus there was stamina in the pedigree, but some way back. Rhodes Scholar had been exported to the USA, where he was a failure at stud, Black Tarquin being a rare exception to the general run of his stock.

More favoured in the betting than Alycidon was Solar Slipper (Windsor Slipper-Solar Flower, by Solario), owned by Joe McGrath and trained at Epsom by Nat Smyth. A strong, burly, rather coarse individual, Solar Slipper had been greatly fancied for The Derby, but injured himself on the morning of the race and could not run. Solar Slipper won the Champion Stakes that year, and when Lord Rosebery congratulated his trainer, Nat Smyth, after the race, Nat replied: "I'm the unluckiest bugger in the world, my Lord, I ought to have won the bloody Derby."

After seeing the Princess of Wales' Stakes, I was sure that Alycidon would win The St. Leger, basing this on his pedigree being stouter than that of Black Tarquin. Had the policy, adopted the next year, of running a pacemaker for Alycidon – in fact he had two – been put into practice for The St. Leger, I think he would have beaten Black Tarquin, who won from Alycidon by one-and-a-half lengths. Alycidon was a genuine but lazy horse who always ran in blinkers and needed a blistering pace to enable him to make the most of his stamina. In The St. Leger, he had to make much of the running, and Black Tarquin was able to tap him for speed. The following season the return match came in the Ascot Gold Cup. This time nothing was left to chance in ensuring that the race was truly run, Alycidon being accompanied by two pacemakers, Stockbridge and Benny Lynch. He was ridden as usual by Douglas Smith, a top-class jockey on whose services Lord Derby had first claim. There were seven runners including the pacemakers, but only two horses in it when it came to the final stage of the race, Alycidon and Black Tarquin. Half way up the straight, Black Tarquin's stamina gave out and Alycidon went on to win by five lengths. Alycidon won all his five starts that year, including the stayers' triple-crown of the Ascot Gold Cup, Goodwood Cup and Doncaster Cup, which had not been accomplished since 1879, when Isonomy did the same. The only race in which Alycidon was not at ease was the Goodwood Cup, when the going was hard, which he disliked.

He was unable to stride out with his usual freedom after hitting the front and Harry Wragg, who trained the second, Riding Mill, told me that he thought that if his jockey, Ken Gethin, had held his horse up a bit longer he might have stolen the race on this account. As it was, Alycidon was by far the better horse of the two and the outstanding stayer of the era bred in England.

A stayer of comparable merit was Marcel Boussac's Marsayas II, by Trimdon out of Astronomie, dam also of Caracalla II, Arbar and Asmena. Caracalla II won the Ascot Gold Cup, Prix de l'Arc de Triomphe and the Grand Prix de Paris, Arbar the Ascot Gold, and Asmena The Oaks. In 1946, when Caracalla II won the Gold Cup, Marsayas II won the Goodwood and Doncaster Cups. In France, among other successes, Marsayas II won the Prix du Cadran, the French equivalent of the Ascot Gold Cup, no less than four times. Charlie Elliott told me that at two miles and upwards Marsayas II was a better horse than Caracalla II. A magnificent, big golden chestnut, powerfully and well built, Marsayas II used to grind the opposition to powder through sheer force of stamina. He sired the Ascot Gold Cup winner Macip. The most notable filly of the immediate postwar years was Masaka, owned and bred by the Aga Khan. She was a fine-looking bay, by Nearco out of the Irish Oaks winner, Majideh, by Mahmoud, out of another good mare to carry the Aga's chocolate and green hoops, Qurat-al-Ain, by Buchan out of Royal Minstrel's dam, Harpsichord. The trouble with Masaka was that she was temperamental and, with Nasrullah, caused Frank Butters to remark that though he had trained some good horses by her sire, Nearco, there were occasions when he wished he had never had one in his stable. At times Masaka would not go at all, at others she shone, winning The Oaks, Irish Oaks, Queen Mary Stakes and July Stakes, and being rated at 9st. 2lbs in the Three-Year-Old Free Handicap, in which Black Tarquin had 9st. 6lbs, Alycidon 9st. 4lbs, and Solar Slipper and My Babu 9st. 2lbs. In The Oaks, Masaka was ridden by Billy Nevitt, the Gordon Richards of north country jockeys, and in the Irish Oaks by Aubrey Brabazon, who thrice won the Cheltenham Gold Cup on Cottage Rake and twice the Champion Hurdle on Hatton's Grace whose other Champion Hurdle victory was under Tim Molony, both trained by Vincent O'Brien.

7

ABERNANT AND OTHERS

In 1948 appeared one of the fastest horses of the postwar decade. This was Abernant, a grey colt bred by The Honble Lady Macdonald-Buchanan and raced by her husband, Sir Reginald. Like Tudor Minstrel, he was by Owen Tudor out of a granddaughter of Lady Josephine. The dam of Abernant was Rustom Mahal, by Rustom Pasha out of Mumtaz Mahal, by The Tetrarch out of Lady Josephine. Fred Darling having retired, Abernant went to be trained by Noel Murless. Noel related that Abernant was not a taking yearling, indeed he was back of the knee and had cow hocks which were away from him. Had he not been such a beautiful mover, he would probably have gone up for sale with those yearlings which were not considered good enough to be put into training by Sir Reginald and Lady Macdonald-Buchanan. The decision to keep Abernant was fortunate. In 23 races over three seasons Abernant was only thrice beaten: a head first time out as a two-year-old, a short head by Nimbus in The Two Thousand Guineas and half-a-length in the King's Stand Stakes as a three-year-old by a good sprinter, Tangle, to whom he was giving 23lbs in heavy going. His victories included the National Breeders' Produce Stakes at Sandown, the Champagne Stakes at Doncaster, the Middle Park Stakes, the July Cup (twice) and the Nunthorpe Stakes (twice). He proved a successful, rather than spectacular, sire and his best winners were mostly fillies. Abernant was always ridden by Gordon Richards and his duel with Nimbus, ridden by Charlie Elliott, in the closing stages of The Two Thousand was an epic of racing and jockeyship. In the Champagne Stakes, Abernant had beaten Nimbus by six lengths, a measure which reflected his superiority at six furlongs; but he had no pretentions to staying a truly run race over a mile at classic level. Nimbus, on the other hand, stayed well, though lacking Abernant's speed. The two were drawn on opposite sides of the course, Nimbus on the far side, Abernant on the stands side. Gordon Richards rode a race worthy of the great Danny Maher, making full use of Abernant's speed and holding him together as his stamina ebbed with each stride nearing the winning post, only letting him down in a final, late effort. Elliott knew that Abernant was the chief danger to Nimbus, and that he had to get across to race with him, but realised that if he cut sharply across he would lose two or three lengths doing so and that his only hope was to move across gradually, arriving to join Abernant in about the last fifty yards. This he did and beat him in the final stride. In The Derby, Elliott again showed himself a master of tactics. Since Nimbus was out of the sprinting mare Kong, a number of critics thought that he might not stay The Derby course and were thus perturbed to see him take up the running from the start. Appreciating that the speed at which the race was being run was not excessive, Eliott went to the front so that he could dictate the pace. Coming round Tattenham Corner he forced Doug Smith on Swallow Tail to swing wide, and half-way up the straight he gradually drifted away from the rails, slightly unbalancing Swallow Tail in doing so and making Johnstone on the fast-finishing Amour Drake switch to the inside, losing a length or so in the operation. In the later days of the head-on camera, Nimbus would have lost the race, but with no such monitor in use, gamesmanship was a necessary part of a jockey's repertoire and in this Charlie Elliott was an adept.

The background to the career of Nimbus is one of the many bizarre stories with which Turf history abounds. Nimbus was bred by the late William Hill, founder of the bookmaking firm of that name and a successful owner and breeder, who won The St. Leger with his home-bred filly Cantelo, by Hills' own horse, Chanteur II, out of Rustic Bridge, by Bois Roussel. Winner of eight races, Cantelo also ran second to Petite Etoile in The Oaks. By Nearco out of Kong, by the Irish Two Thousand and Derby winner Baytown, Nimbus was sold as a yearling from Hills' Whitsbury Manor Stud, being knocked down to George Colling for 5,000 guineas on behalf of H. Glenister, a newcomer to racing, who gave the horse to his wife. Nimbus was a big, powerful bay colt, with great heart room and good limbs, though his hocks were a bit away from him. His buyer was in charge of a trustee department of the Midland Bank, a position which did not seem sufficiently remunerative to entitle him to own racehorses. That he did so, it was generally believed, was due to his wife having money, weight being added to this theory by the fact that

Nimbus ran in Mrs Glenister's name. The truth finally emerged after Glenister committed suicide in 1952, grave financial discrepancies having been discovered in his department of the bank. Glenister did not bet, but when Nimbus won The Two Thousand Guineas and most critics, as well as bookmakers, derided the horse's chance in The Derby on the grounds that he was unlikely to stay the distance, Glenister was so incensed at this denigration of his favourite that he had a large bet on Nimbus to win The Derby and had the satisfaction of being proved right.

Luck was certainly on Glenister's side in The Derby. Apart from Elliott's skill in the race and there being no objection to Nimbus interfering with Amour Drake, the presence of Jack Jarvis may have forestalled defeat. George Colling, trainer of Nimbus, was too ill to go to Epsom and asked Jack Jarvis to take charge of proceedings in his place. When Jarvis went to saddle Nimbus he found him being ridden by a fairly heavy lad, perhaps because the one leading him, or the travelling head lad, was frightened of the horse getting loose, being big, strong and full of himself. Knowing the disadvantage to a horse having weight on his back for some time before a race – wise jockeys invariably dismount if there is a delay at the post – Jarvis ordered the lad off the horse's back, judging the chances of his getting loose to be the lesser of two evils. In view of Nimbus's narrow victory this decision might have been the deciding factor.

I met Glenister once, on the July course at Newmarket, and had a long talk with him about breeding, in which he was greatly interested. Tall, goodlooking, with glasses, he had a studious appearance and was agreeable company. He had a sound theoretical knowledge of breeding, but little or no understanding of the practical side, and I recall Reg Day, who managed Nimbus at stud, complaining that some of the mares chosen by Glenister as mates for Nimbus, on theoretical grounds, were quite unsuitable physically. Nimbus proved a disappointment at stud as compared with his half-brother Grey Sovereign (Nasrullah – Kong). His best winners were Nagami (Coronation Cup, third in the triple-crown), Nucleus (Jockey Club Stakes, second in St. Leger), Watteau, a good horse in Italy, and the French 1,000 Guineas winner Nubile.

Having trained Nimbus, George Colling was naturally interested in his half-brother, by Nasrullah, (later to be named Grey Sovereign), when he came up as a yearling. A grey, built more on the lines of a sprinter than Nimbus, the yearling turned Colling out of the box when he went to inspect the colt at the sales. As a result, Colling did not buy him and he was knocked down to his eventual trainer, George Beeby, under whose care Grey Sovereign became a top-class sprinter. At stud Grey Sovereign proved far more successful than Nimbus, becoming a powerful name in the modern thoroughbred. George Beeby once said to me that, at that time, he had no starting gate on his training ground; in spite of this, Harry Carr, who rode for him whenever he was not claimed by Cecil Boyd-Rochfort – for whom he won The Derby on Parthia, The One Thousand, Oaks and Leger on Meld, and The Leger and King George VI and the Queen Elizabeth Stakes on Alcide – remarked how good his horses were at the starting gate. Beeby attributed this to all his horses being made to lead the string in turn.

Of The Derby winners of this period, I rate Pinza (Chanteur II-Pasqua, by Manna) the best. A big, strong, rather coarse individual, somewhat straight in front – he eventually broke down – he was bred by Fred Darling, who sold him at the Newmarket July Sales to Sir Victor Sassoon for 1,500 guineas. I had got to know Fred Darling quite well, having ridden a winner for him just before the war and as a result of his approaching me regarding the possibility of succeeding him at Beckhampton, and used to go over to see him fairly often. By then he was an invalid, but took a keen interest in his stud, his horses in training with Noel Murless and racing in general, and kindly used to invite me to look at his yearlings and discuss them with him. Pinza impressed me, except for his forelegs, which looked as if they would not carry his big weight through much racing without the risk of breaking down. In view of this it seemed unlikely that Pinza would make a high price at the sales, and I mentioned this to George Todd, suggesting that he bought him and cut him, with a view to bringing off a gamble in one of the important handicaps. Had this procedure been followed, some of the bookmakers would have suffered. As it was, at two Pinza, who was trained by Norman Bertie, formerly Fred Darling's head lad, won the Tattersall Sales Stakes and the Dewhurst, running second in the Royal Lodge Stakes to the late Aga Khan's filly Neemah (Migoli-Naishapur, by Nearco), who relished the soft going to which Pinza was unsuited. The following season Pinza was unbeaten in his three races, the Newmarket Stakes, The Derby and the King George VI and the Queen Elizabeth Stakes. In the latter two races Pinza beat the Queen's good colt Aureole (Hyperion-Angelola, by Donatello II), who won the race the following year and had finished second to Pinza in The Derby. Henry Porchester (now Earl of Carnarvon), who gave me a lift home after the Newmarket Stakes, and I were so impressed by Pinza's victory that we agreed he would win The Derby and backed him.

Jack Clayton, who owned and managed the Bedford Lodge Stables where Pinza was trained, was a delightful, aristocratic-looking man. Tall, slim, with a faintly unobtrusive, light-coloured moustache. He was injured – I think playing football at Eton – as a boy, as a result of which he could not play further games and was not A1 medically, but managed to serve in the Welsh Guards during the war. Like his sister, Jane, he never married, and they shared the trainers house at Bedford Lodge now occupied by Luca Cumani.

The family originally came from Northumberland, but Jack, an inveterate gambler, lost a fortune betting and the property had to be sold. Indeed, had not some of his friends at Oxford forced him to put aside a fairly substantial sum of money in a Trust which he could not touch, he might have bankrupted himself. As it turned out, he curbed his betting, and always had a horse or two in training. Before the war, Jack acted as racing manager to James V. Rank and for him had a steady run of success. Jack's own stable, which started soon after the 1939–45 war, did fairly well: he was fond of his horses and gave me the impression that they tended to be under-worked. After Pinza, his best horse from the stable was The One Thousand Guineas winner of 1951, Belle of All. Jack died after a short illness in 1975, aged 72.

I would rate Never Say Die (Nasrullah-Singing Grass, by War Admiral) the next best Derby winner of the period, ahead of Tulyar (Tehran-Neocracy, by Nearco), who was lucky in striking a moderate year and having the advantage of Smirke's jockeyship. Never Say Die, owned and bred by the American, Mr. R.S. Clark, for many years a loyal supporter of English racing, who generously presented the horse to the National Stud at the end of his racing career, was trained at Newmarket by Joe Lawson, former head lad to Alec Taylor at Manton. Bearing no resemblance to his sire Nasrullah, either in looks or temperament, Never Say Die was an out-and-out stayer; so much so that in the final gallop before The St. Leger, on Yarmouth racecourse, which he won by many lengths in a canter, it was found that by mistake the horses went two miles. Never Say Die was burly, phlegmatic and chestnut – his sire Nasrullah was refined, highly strung and bay – and, though winning at six furlongs as a two-year-old, the further he went the more impressive he was: he won The Derby by an easy two lengths, ridden by Lester Piggott, The St. Leger by twelve lengths in the hands of Charlie Smirke, as Piggott was under suspension over his riding of Never Say Die in a rough race for the King Edward VII Stakes at Royal Ascot, won by Rashleigh, in which Never Say Die finished fourth. Never Say Die proved quite a successful sire, probably the best horse by him being the One Thousand and Oaks winner of 1960, Never Too Late II, a beautiful chestnut filly out of Gloria Nicky, by Alycidon from the sprinter Weighbridge. Though Never Say Die's son Larkspur won The Derby he was not a good horse, his victory being due to his avoiding a pile-up in the race, during which the probable winner, Hethersett (Hugh Lupus-Bride Elect, by Big Game), later to win The St. Leger, was brought down. In his old age Never Say Die became extremely coarse, looking more like a half-bred than a thoroughbred, but he has left his mark on the breed, and appears in the pedigrees of many important winners.

No Derby winner of this period approached the brilliance of Dante, successful in 1945 at Newmarket during the war. Bred and owned by Sir Eric Ollson, Dante became a red-hot favourite for The St. Leger, ante-post money pouring on him. Then, suddenly, he was scratched. It was known that he had been having trouble with his eyesight, but this seemed to have been arrested by treatment, and when later it was announced that he had gone blind it came as a shock to the public. There was an undercurrent of feeling that something was not quite right about the whole business, but nothing emerged to clear the matter up, till one day, not long before he died, the late Richard Scrope, an old friend of mine, told me how he chanced on the truth. This, as he related it to me, is that one day he went to see his oculist in London, who said to him: "You're a racing man, so this will interest you. I was rung up one day by a Mr. Peacock, who explained that he had charge of a very good race-horse, who seemed to be developing defective eyesight, and the owner would like me to examine the horse, to see if I could diagnose the trouble and treat it. I went up to Middleham, looked at the horse's eyes and found that his sight was imperfect but could be stabilised by regular applications of eye-drops, which I supplied. Some months later Mr. Peacock telephoned to say that the drops would not longer be required. I made it clear to him that if the treatment ceased the horse would go blind, to which he replied: 'These are my instructions' and the inevitable happened." It is not a pleasant story and all concerned are dead, but it is part of Turf history and, like other of its blacker aspects, should be known. Dante, though by then quite blind, did fairly well at stud and sired the 2000 Guineas winner, Darius. Dante died in 1956, aged 14.

The outstanding middle-distance horse of the period was the Italian-bred Ribot, unbeaten in sixteen races, winner of the Prix de l'Arc de Triomphe twice, of the King George VI and the Queen Elizabeth Stakes and most of the top races in Italy. He was bred by the great Federico

Tesio, who died before Ribot raced, and was by Tenerani out of Romanella, by El Greco. Ribot was the perfect racing machine. Bay with no white about him, he was about 16 hands and technically faultless, though critics rated him plain, perhaps because he lacked the refined head of some thoroughbreds and did not show himself off well except in action, when he moved superbly. He would not have beaten Tudor Minstrel at a mile, or Abernant at six furlongs, but at one-and-a-half miles nothing then could live with him, whatever the going. After a brief period at stud in England and Italy Ribot went to the USA, where he proved a top-class sire and an important influence.

Of the notable English fillies of the time, the best were Masaka, of whom I have written already, and Meld (Alycidon-Daily Double, by Fair Trial), winner of the One Thousand, Oaks and St. Leger. Bred and owned by Lady Zia Wernher, trained by Cecil Boyd-Rochfort, and ridden by Harry Carr, Meld was a beautiful big filly, hard to fault, going back to the famous taproot Double Life.

Also worthy of mention are the two French-trained fillies, Coronation V (Djebel-Esmerelda, by Tourbillon) and Bella Paola (Ticino-Rhea II, by Gundomar). Coronation V, a tall attractive individual, bred and owned by Marcel Boussac, was closely inbred to Tourbillon, sire of both Djebel and Esmerelda, and won the Queen Mary Stakes, French 1,000 Guineas and Prix de l'Arc de Triomphe. She was a bad traveller, which almost certainly accounted for her defeats in The Oaks, by Musidora, in The Irish Oaks and the Queen Elizabeth II Stakes. Coronation V never got in foal, which I believe was for a physical reason and nothing to do with her inbreeding. Bella Paola, whose pedigree was almost entirely German, was a strong, well-made filly, in her dark brown coat with no trace of white marking, general build and placid temperament typical of the German thoroughbred at its best. A top-class winner in France, Bella Paola also won the One Thousand, Oaks and Champion Stakes. Her owner-breeder was Francois Dupré, for whose stud she founded a successful family, now represented in the Aga Khan's bloodstock.

8

TRAINERS AND JOCKEYS

Fred Darling and Frank Butters, who have been mentioned in this story, belong chiefly to an earlier period. The finest trainer to succeed them was Noel Murless, a genius. I knew Noel from his early days at Hambledon, when he trained a small mixed string, and had a couple of rides for him – both finished last – and later at Beckhampton and up to his death at Newmarket. His record is there for posterity, so does not need repeating. The outstanding skill of Noel Murless was founded on uncanny understanding of horses, great patience, excellent stable management and attention to detail. An example of his flair was brought home to me through a filly named Hardiesse, by Hornbeam out of Stage Fright, by Big Game. She belonged to Harry Oppenheimer, for whom I was then managing his horses in training in England, and for whom I had bought Stage Fright, carrying Hardiesse, to fill a nomination for which he did not want an expensive mare. As a yearling Hardiesse was a nice filly, but her sire Hornbeam was not popular and her dam Stage Fright had not bred any horse of distinction; so I was somewhat diffident about approaching Noel to take Hardiesse to train. However he agreed and when in the February of her two-year-old career I asked Noel how Hardiesse was getting on, to my astonishment, since he never got at his two-year-olds early, he replied: "I think she'll be my Oaks filly." In due course Hardiesse won the second of her two races in her first season, and in her next, was successful in three good races out of five starts and, what is more, was fourth in The Oaks when badly in season, but for which she would certainly have been placed. Like Fred Darling, Noel Murless was autocratic with owners, his horses always coming first: he once forgot to let Jim Joel know that he was running a horse in a good handicap, which he won; and on one occasion John Howard de Walden (Lord Howard de Walden) was constrained to observe to him with regard to running Magic Flute in the Coronation Stakes at Royal Ascot, which she won, despite Murless not wishing to run her. "If I owned her she'd run." The death of Jim Joel left Lord Howard de Walden as the last of the great traditional English owner-breeders. Inheriting his stud from his father, the 8th Baron who died in 1946, John Howard de Walden was born in 1912 and developed a penchant for racing at Cambridge, where he was a contemporary of a number of keen followers of the Turf among them the late Tom Blackwell and John Abergavenny (then the Honble John Nevill) and who both later became members of the Jockey Club. After the death of his father, he developed his racing and breeding interests on sound and imaginative lines, being about the first breeder to appreciate the value of stout German blood with the help of which he bred his best horse, The Derby winner Slip Anchor, now a highly successful sire.

Having a quiet, pertinent and effective wit and a certain, agreeable sense of the ridiculous which his stint as Senior Steward of the Jockey Club and other official burdens have failed to diminish, he has never taken life, himself, – or racing, too seriously. His recent autobiography 'Earls Have Peacocks', which touches only lightly on the Turf, reflects these pleasant traits. Since Noel Murless's death his chief trainer has been Henry Cecil at Murless's old stable, Warren Place, Newmarket.

Noel's prototype in Ireland was Vincent O'Brien who, like Noel, started with jumpers, but remained longer in this milieu, reaching the top before attaining similar status on the flat. Vincent O'Brien's status as a trainer can be judged by having trained 6 Derby winners, 2 Oaks winners, 3 St. Leger winners, 4 winners of The Two Thousand, 1 of The One Thousand and some of the most important events in Ireland and France.

The period under review marks the end of that phase of Turf history which started with the introduction of the American seat and ended before the fashion of riding with ultra-short stirrup leathers was introduced in the 1960s by Lester Piggott. At that time the barrier start had not been replaced by stalls; flat-race jockeys wore neither crash helmets nor goggles, or body protectors; there was no overnight declaration of runners; motorways had not come into being – racegoers travelled mostly by train and usually stayed away for the whole of a three or four-day meeting; hundred-horse stables were unknown; discipline was stricter and standards higher among stable lads, and stable-girls became commonplace in virtually every yard. In the immediate post-war years, entry to the members' enclosure on racecourses and to the Royal Enclosure at Ascot was restricted and socially biased: to enter the members' at Newmarket it was necessary to obtain a voucher signed by *two* members of the Jockey Club, and licensed trainers were not accepted as members unless they had joined before taking out a licence; divorced people were banned from the Royal Enclosure at Ascot; there were few commoners in the Jockey Club. Extensive buying of yearlings in the USA had not begun; the Grand National fences had not been modified; all-weather racing was undreamt of, as was Arab involvement; comparatively few English horses ran abroad; sponsorship was rare; several important racecourses, now defunct, such as Birmingham, Manchester and Derby, were still in use; there was no night racing; Ascot's course and stands had not been altered; the photo-finish, patrol camera and technology in general were in their infancy or non-existent; and other changes which escape the memory had not yet come about.

The golden age of jockeyship, which began with Danny Maher and Frank Wootton, continuing with Steve Donoghue and others such as Frank Bullock, Brownie Carslake, Freddy Fox and Harry Wragg, was drawing to a close. Gordon Richards, Charlie Smirke, Charlie Elliott, Tommy Weston, Michael Beary, and the brothers Eph and Doug Smith were about the last eminent representatives of that era still riding. Lester Piggott came on the scene as an apprentice, but had not yet adopted the style of riding with ultra-short stirrup-leathers which is now the fashion. Of the younger jockeys, the best and most stylish were Joe and Manny Mercer; another was Jimmy Lindley, a good rider of the classic school, who was a product of Tom Masson's tuition, also responsible for Bobby Elliott. Lindley had a successful spell over hurdles when troubled by weight problems. Following those earlier, fine Australian jockeys, Frank Bullock and Brownie Carslake, came the later invasion from 'Down Under', represented chiefly by Scobie Breasley, Edgar Britt, George Cook, Bill Williamson, Ron Hutchinson and, later, George Moore. All were good riders, though Williamson and Hutchinson suffered the disadvantage of being unable to use the whip left-handed, which lost them races. Breasley, Britt and Cook were particularly effective: neat, cool, good tacticians, well-balanced and sympathetic to horses, they rode with medium-length leathers, a shortish rein, always maintaining contact with the horse's mouth, and were excellent judges of pace. The greatest all-round jockey and finest character in the profession of my time was Gordon Richards; the best classic jockeys were Smirke, Elliott and Piggott, who surpassed Richards in this sphere in the matter of temperament, being ice-cool while Richards was highly-strung. Had I to name one jockey as the best in pure technical ability and on the big day, it would be Smirke, the choice also of Stanley Wootton, the greatest producer of jockeys in Turf history, with whom Smirke served his time.

The standard of flat-race riding was higher then than it is now. In those days jockeys virtually never fell off on the flat, which is by no means unknown nowadays. They kept horses straighter and seldom lost races through using the whip in the wrong hand, which is no rarity today, even with top jockeys. Though the rules governing the use of the whip were more lax formerly and some jockeys were unduly severe in the use of it, most could get more out of horses with hands and heels only, than is possible today, when riding so short precludes the use of a rider's legs as a means of propulsion and guidance. A scientific examination of the theory of the flat-racing seat reveals that once the rider's centre of gravity is placed above or slightly in front of that of the horse, which was achieved by the length of leathers used in the 'golden era', there is no point in riding any shorter. In fact, the modern fashion can prove a hindrance: for instance, sitting down in the saddle with the body more or less upright, thus placing the rider's weight too far back and attracting unnecessary wind-resistance, as modern jockeys are sometimes depicted. On a free-running horse who goes straight and does nothing wrong, a jockey can ride as short as he likes, provided he sits still, has his weight in the right place and his body positioned to avoid wind-resistance; but when horses hang, swerve, roll or otherwise cause problems, the shorter the leathers above the scientific norm, the harder it is to keep a horse on an even keel, running straight, the rider's weight where it should be and, in some circumstances, himself on the horse.

In the jumping world, the period was one of exceptionally good riders: Bryan Marshall, Fred Winter, Martin and Tim Molony, Fred Rimell and Aubrey Brabazon being perhaps the best. On the flat, Martin Molony and Aubrey Brabazon rode classic winners, Fred Rimell had 40 winners before getting heavy and Bryan Marshall, who served his time with Atty Persse, and Fred Winter both rode winners under JC Rules before weight caught up with them. My choice of the best among this exceptionally talented group is Bryan Marshall, more elegant than Fred Winter and the Molony brothers, stronger than Aubrey Brabazon and tactically superior to Fred Rimell. Over hurdles, Johnny Gilbert and Harry Sprague stand out as the natural successors to George Duller and Staff Ingham. As related, Vincent O'Brien was an outstanding N.H. trainer, heading the list twice, before confining himself to the flat. The most successful N.H.

trainer in England during these years was Fulke Walwyn, who headed the list in 1946–7, 1947–8 and 1948–9. Of the N.H. horses, four stand out: the magnificent Prince Regent, winner of the Cheltenham Gold Cup in 1946 at the age of 11 and third in the 'National under 12st. 5lbs the same year, trained by Tom Dreaper and ridden by Tim Hyde; Cottage Rake, three times winner of the Cheltenham Gold Cup, trained by Vincent O'Brien and ridden by Aubrey Brabazon; and the treble Champion Hurdle winner, Sir Ken, ridden by Tim Molony and trained by Willie Stephenson, who also sent out a 'National winner in Oxo and a Derby winner in Arctic Prince; and Hatton's Grace, winner of three champion Hurdles (two ridden by Aubrey Brabazon and one by Tim Molony), whose trainer Vincent O'Brien has the remarkable record of having sent out three consecutive winners of the 'National, Early Mist, Royal Tan and Quare Times, the first two ridden by Bryan Marshall, the other by Pat Taafe, and the six Derby winners, Larkspur, ridden by the Australian Neville Selwood, later killed riding in France, Sir Ivor, Nijinksy, Roberto, The Minstrel, all ridden by Lester Piggott, and Golden Fleece, partnered by Pat Eddery. Though he never rode him, it is interesting that Lester Piggott once remarked that he thought that Golden Fleece was possibly the best of the lot.

Of the 'chasers of my time, I class Easter Hero, Golden Miller, Prince Regent and Arkle as the greatest. Arkle and Easter Hero were the most brilliant, but as the former was never asked to face the gruelling task of jumping Aintree, for me Easter Hero deserves the palm.

9

A FRIEND AND A COUP

One day in 1949 I had a telephone call from a former brother officer in Phantom, Tony Loughborough (The Earl of Rosslyn). We had been in different squadrons, so did not see much of each other, but met periodically at RHQ, which was at Richmond in Surrey, our officers' mess being at Pembroke Lodge in Richmond Park. So the call came as rather a surprise, likewise its import. This was to say that he was interested in buying a racehorse and wanted to know what it would cost. I explained that while there would be no difficulty in finding the horse, the price would depend on its quality, and suggested that as few racehorses pay their way it would probably be best for me to try to find a cheap one and for us to go halves in it, thus cutting down any possible loss to a minimum. Tony thought this an excellent idea and asked me to go ahead with the project. Though Tony had never been concerned with horses or racing, his grandfather, the 5th Earl, from whom he inherited the title, was well known on the Turf as something of an eccentric and fearless gambler, who originally raced as Mr. Herringbone under the bizarre colours of 'white, black skull and crossbones, black cap'. These must have been discarded as in Tony's day the family colours were 'bronze, turquoise sleeves and cap', which were the same as my father's in India and thus were not available when I applied for them in England. The Rosslyn second colours were 'pink, green collar and cuffs', which Tony used, because his cousin, 'Boo' Henderson, had the first colours and asked to keep them, thinking it unlucky to change. The disappearance of the skull and crossbones may have been due to the refusal of the jockey Jack Watts to wear them, on the grounds that "race riding was quite dangerous enough without wearing those colours."

102

Jean and I got to know and like Tony well. He was a stimulating character, always in good spirits, amusing, generous, good company, with not too serious a view of life and himself. "I say all the wrong things like 'phone,', 'couch' and 'lounge'." He was a good mixer and completely un-class-conscious – when being shown round a friend's garden he disconcerted the gardener and surprised his friend by offering the former a cigarette; – treated his old butler, John, more as an equal than a servant, and always had a cheerful word for the lad in charge of his horse, making sure he knew his name. It came as a terrible shock to us and to all who knew Tony when some years later, for no discernible reason, he took his own life. Apparently, he suffered periodically from acute depression, which he concealed from the outside world. Shortly before his death he came to live near Newbury and I telephoned him to ask him to dinner. He seemed as ebullient as ever and answered: "I'd love to, old boy, but can't at the moment, the house is being done up and hasn't got a front door. As soon as it's fixed I'll ring you and we'll arrange something." It was the last time we spoke together.

It was early in the year that Tony called me about finding him a horse. I consulted Tom Masson on the matter, and he told me that he knew of an unbroken filly belonging to a farmer, John Craig, near Lewes, which he thought could be bought cheaply. We went to see her and liked her. She was a darkish bay, strongly made, a typical sprinter, with powerful quarters, well-sprung ribs, a nicely sloped shoulder, clean, well-formed limbs and an intelligent, bold head; if she was to be faulted, it was that she had slightly bent hocks, a trait often found in fast horses, but less frequently in stayers. We bought her on the spot for about £250. Tony was thrilled when we told him and decided to call her 'Madame Bovary', after the chief character in Flaubert's novel of that title. I don't know what inspired his choice, as the filly's pedigree had no connection with the name; she was by Linklater out of Buck Bean, by Duke of Buckingham out of Lady Mere, winner of three races and dam of eight winners, including Lady of Shallott, a good filly who won at Royal Ascot, and Merely a Minor, winner of ten races. Had Madame Bovary been offered at one of the yearling sales, well presented, she would have made a good deal more than we gave for her.

Coming into training at this late stage, instead of in September or October when most yearlings are broken, and having been running out in a field, Madame Bovary was backward compared with most other two-year-olds. However, Tom Masson, to whom she went to be trained at Lewes, got on with her and, in order to give her some experience of racing, she ran a couple of times in April, in a maiden plate at Hurst Park and a selling race at Epsom, unplaced. She did not appear again until late August, when she finished fourth in a selling race at Brighton and fifth in a similar race at Lewes. This showed that she was improving, though still short of her potential. By October she had come on sufficiently to have an each-way chance in a selling nursery at Warwick, in which she was set to carry 7st. 13lbs, being ridden by one of Tom Masson's apprentices, Carol Orton. We backed her win and place at 7–1 and she was beaten a head for second place. Madame Bovary's final race that season was in another selling nursery, at Windsor in November. Ridden this time by the top-class jockey Doug Smith and backed each way at 10–1, she finished second. Her steady improvement throughout the season was encouraging; though she failed to win, our two bets showed a profit and there was every hope that she would do even better the following season.

Madame Bovary thrived during the winter and reappeared in 1950 in the Copper Horse Handicap, 6 furlongs for 3-year-olds, at Windsor. The class was too high for her, but we wanted to give her a race as part of her preparation for a gamble in a seller. Ridden by Orton she finished unplaced, but ran well enough to show that she had improved. The race chosen for our proposed coup was the Erdington Maiden 3-year-old Selling Handicap, 6 furlongs, at Birmingham on May 30th 1950; but before the day it was important to find out, exactly, if she merited a serious bet. This presented a problem since Tom Masson's stable comprised almost entirely jumpers – the previous season our assessment of Madame Bovary had been largely guesswork, based on her races in public and her general wellbeing, but this time we needed more accurate information. The solution was found through Victor Smyth, the trainer whose charge, the subsequent Champion Hurdle winner National Spirit, carried me to victory at Fontwell. Having had the position explained to him, he proposed that we should try Madame Bovary at Kempton Park with a couple of horses from his stable at weights which, if the gallop came out in favour of our filly, would virtually ensure her success at Birmingham. We agreed to this suggestion gratefully and set about making the necessary arrangements. Vic Smyth said that he would provide two horses with recent form – one of them was Full Blast, who had finished third in the Yarborough 3-year-old Handicap, 6 furlongs, carrying 8st. 5lbs, at Lincoln. He did not want to know the name of our horse but, if the result of the gallop was satisfactory, would like a 'pony' on with us on the day. Orton was to ride Madame Bovary in the trial and

A short head victory for Pont Cordonnier (J.H.) from the favourite Red Pippin (Alan Oughton) after a drawn out battle at Lewes.

Stipend (J.H.) nearest camera at the last hurdle before winning from Welsh Pet (David Punshon) here in front and Valastro (S. Maundrell) at Windsor.

Maisey Hampton (J.H.) a comfortable winner at Lewes from La Jacobin (Alan Oughton), Sylvain II (P. Herbert) and Noble Bill (E. Underwood).

J.H. with senior Jockey Club handicapper Geoffrey Freer
watching racing at York.

be in charge of her in the horse-box – her lad, John Ciechanowski, a pupil in the stable and later champion amateur rider of Europe, stayed at home, on the principle that the fewer in the know the better. Orton and the horse-box driver were told that on no account were they to divulge Madame Bovary's name to Vic Smyth's lads; the latter tried to discover it but failed. Jean, I and my mother-in-law, who for some reason came with us but for security was left in the car during the trial, set out for Kempton, arriving well before the appointed time of 8 a.m. The teams from each stable were also punctual, the horses were unboxed, sorted themselves out, walked round for a short time, then cantered down to the 6-furlong start, this being the distance over which they were to be tried. They broke evenly, came a real good gallop and Madame Bovary won comfortably. It was an encouraging result and we were able to enjoy breakfast at the Mitre Hotel at Hampton Court in the knowledge that, bar accident, we had a racing certainty at Birmingham. The trial took place about a week before the race and Madame Bovary came out of it well, eating up afterwards and continuing to thrive. Tony was thrilled when we reported the outcome of the gallop, and asked how the procedure for backing her was to be worked. In those days, before the introduction of the betting tax, there were a number of professional backers who made their living by working commissions for owners and trainers and backing horses themselves. When the betting tax was introduced they disappeared, because the mathematical odds became so stacked against winning by day-to-day betting that the risk of losing was not justified. With the removal of the tax on betting on the racecourse in 1987, they began to reappear. One of the most respected of these operators at the time was Pierre Higgins. Then in late middle age, he used to do commissions for such eminent trainers as Cecil Boyd-Rochfort, Atty Pierce, Jack Colling, and their patrons. Not being a serious gambler, I had never made use of his services, but knew him well as a regular racegoer and decided that he was the man for the job. Pierre, or Peter as most racegoers called him, came from the north, Manchester I think, and looked most unlike a racing man, resembling more a lay preacher or a clergyman out of uniform, with always a dark suit, sombre shirt and tie, and grey homburg. It was said that he invariably carried a Bible in his pocket. Of medium, square build and clean shaven, his features, which slightly resembled those of the one-time Prime Minister Stanley Baldwin, fitted his general appearance, but he was full of humour, scrupulously honest and had a warm and generous nature: when war broke out he sent the Government a large sum of money towards the war effort; and Jack Colling told me that, in his latter years, Peter once paid out the proceeds of quite a substantial bet which, Jack discovered, he had forgotten to place but later remembered. His wife usually went racing with him; she was a neat, unobtrusive little woman, dressed in black, who sat quietly by herself while her husband was involved in the hurly-burly of the rails and the betting ring. Nico Collin, a hunting and racing friend from my pre-war days in Sussex, who has the best store of racing anecdotes of anyone I know, told me one concerning Cecil Boyd-Rochfort and Peter Higgins, to which he was a witness. Nico was on the stands at York, near Cecil. The latter liked the general public to think that he was not concerned with betting, though in fact he was a shrewd and successful backer of the horses he trained. On this occasion he had a runner in the race about to take place and a friend standing by him said, "How will yours go here, Cecil?", to which the latter replied, "Only a lunatic would have a bet in a race of this kind". At this moment Peter Higgins appeared at the foot of the stands and, to Cecil's discomfiture, called up to him, "I've got you seven to two to the lot, Captain." Returning to Madame Bovary, I approached Peter and asked him if he could back a horse for us at Birmingham, naming the day and the race, saying that I would see him on the course to confirm the details, to which he agreed. I cannot remember the amount of the total commission, but Tony had £400 each way and I had £400 to win and £200 a place.

As the day approached, Tony got more and more excited. He wondered if he should wear a hat, which he never did, and possibly a false moustache because, if he was recognised, and having a runner, people might put two and two together, step in and pinch the market. Since he never went racing and few racegoers would know him, I assured him that this would not be necessary. For some reason Jean did not come to Birmingham, so Tony and I set out together. He was then living with his mother at Bracknell, which had not yet been developed into the monstrosity of a new town, thus he was within easy access of us at East Woodhay House. Tony drove me in his car. It was a mild dull day, but dry and we had a pleasant drive, Tony bubbling over with excitement, I somewhat on edge as was always the case before a race in which I was concerned, rather more so this time since the money involved was by far my largest bet. Birmingham racecourse, which has long since disappeared beneath a motorway and buildings, was one of the best courses in the country; Charlie Elliott used to say it was the only decent course in England. Ours was the second race, so we had ample time for a sandwich and a drink to calm our nerves. The top class jockey, Eph

Smith, who won The Derby on Blue Peter, was engaged for Madame Bovary, who was set to carry 7st. 13lbs. We found Peter Higgins and told him the amount of the commission, having first met Tom Masson and learned that Madame Bovary was in good order. There were fourteen runners, not one of which had been placed in its previous race, so the opposition was weak and the only possible danger lay in bad luck. Peter Higgins had a couple of other horses to back in the race and placed these bets before backing Madame Bovary: as a result he got us a good price and she eventually started favourite at 7–2. The race can be summed up best by the comment in Raceform: "looked well, made all", Madame Bovary jumping off in front, was never headed and won by three lengths.

Being a 'seller', our filly had to come up for auction after the race, which was worth £277 to the winner, the selling price being, so far as I recall, £100; this meant that, if we bought her in, anything over £377 would represent a loss, apart from our bets. As it was we got her back for £350, but might have had to go more if the late Lord Willoughby de Broke, who had started to bid for her because he once owned a successful member of the family, and was a friend, had not realised that I owned a share in her and when he saw me bidding dropped out. After it was all over, Peter Higgins came up to me and said: "I had a feeling this was going to win so I brought my cheque-book with me. We'll go into the bar and have a glass of champagne and I'll pay you." We did so and Peter wrote me out a cheque for just on £10,000, an agreeable and satisfactory outcome to the operation. Madame Bovary never won again, but we did not give the bookmakers back their money, as we only backed her again once, for a modest amount each way. This was the following year, when she finished second in a selling handicap at Worcester, beaten a length and a half by a 20–1 outsider ridden by Lester Piggott, Palm Grove. The latter had never been placed in seven previous races, but had not been running in selling races and was receiving 8lbs from Madame Bovary, so was rather better than the weight she carried suggested. After winning in 1950, Madame Bovary ran twice unplaced and finished second and fourth in small, non-selling handicaps. She then went to stud where she bred six winners, all by cheap sires. Of these, Holy Deadlock (by Nomellini) won 12 races, Allumeuse (by Falls of Clyde) and Zeno (by Zimone) six each, while Apollo Boy, a handsome colt by Ratification, was a good winner abroad after a single success in England.

Fired by our success with Madame Bovary, Tony suggested in 1951 that we should take a chance with another horse. I knew of nothing for sale privately, so decided to try the Dublin yearling sales, on the principle that they would probably offer a wider choice at our price than the sales at Newmarket or Doncaster; so Tom Masson and I went over together to Ireland to see what we could find. Our price was in the £500–£600 bracket and we wanted a yearling likely to win as a two-year-old. A colt by Golden Cloud out of Suilvaun, by Sir Walter Raleigh caught my eye. A golden chestnut with a flaxen mane and tail, he was on the small side, but well made, strong, active and had an attractive head, big eye and a kind intelligent expression. His worst feature was his feet, which were rather shelly but adequate. He looked all over a sprinter that would come to hand early. Tom Masson approved him and he was knocked down to me for 550 guineas. We named him Cloud of Glory. Since Cloud of Glory had cost only 550 guineas, he was eligible for certain races confined to horses which had been bought at public auctions for less than a stated sum. One such was the Manton Stakes at Newbury on April 19th 1952, and we decided to make this our objective. By this time Tom Masson had more flat racers in his stable, so there was no need to go outside for trial tackle. Two horses in particular fitted the bill, a three-year-old gelding named Battle Flat, who had some selling plate form the previous year and had improved – subsequently he won a couple of moderate handicaps – and a nice little two-year-old gelding of my own, by Mazarin, named Newman, whom I had bought cheaply as a yearling, but who moved well. Newman was entered in a selling plate at Newbury on the day before Cloud of Glory's race and this gave us a line to the latter's chance, the two having worked together. We galloped Newman and Battle Flat with Cloud of Glory, putting the last named in at dis-advantageous terms, over three furlongs in mid-February, over four furlongs in March and over five furlongs a fortnight before his race. He won each gallop convincingly.

The auspices looked favourable when Newman ran fourth of 23 in the selling plate on the previous day, as he was a stone and an easy beating behind Cloud of Glory. While the latter did not represent the certainty that did Madame Bovary, because only four of the 18 runners had raced, the rest being unknown quantities, Cloud of Glory was worth a bet and we invested accordingly; so far as I recall my bet was £200, to win only. This time we gave the commission to Major Charlie Moss MC, a regular racegoer for whom I had ridden a winner and who was to some extent a professional backer, Peter Higgins not being at the meeting. Charlie came up to me before the 'off' to say that he had only been able to get 5–1 as someone had stepped in and taken the cream of the market.

This transpired to be a friend staying with us, who was not content with the amount he agreed to have in the stable bet and forestalled us by having a substantial bet on his own account. The starting price was 4–1. Orton, the stable jockey and by then out of his apprenticeship and an experienced, competent and reliable rider, was on Cloud of Glory and knew him well, having ridden him in all his work. Jimmy Lindley, who succeeded him and went on to greater things, had only recently joined the stable as an apprentice.

Cloud of Glory got a good start and was always in the leading group. He struck the front inside the distance, was headed by Prince Tony close to the winning post, but managed to rally in the last stride and the two passed the post together. We were kept in suspense for some minutes, because the camera was in use for the first time and the judge called for a photo. Cloud of Glory was on the stands side, Prince Tony on his near side. Nowadays it is recognised that in a close finish at Newbury the horse on the stands side usually proves the winner, but then no such evidence existed and the bookmakers, on the judgement of their eyes, were laying 7–1 against Cloud of Glory proving the winner. Fortunately, they suffered an optical illusion: when the verdict came it was a short head in our favour. Cloud of Glory was entered in the Hyde Park Stakes at Epsom four days later. He came out of the Newbury race well, and since he was fit, forward and did not have much scope for improvement, we decided to let him take his chance in the race. Though the opposition was above the class of the Manton Stakes, carried more prestige and a bigger prize, Cloud of Glory would have the advantage of fitness and experience over some of the opposition, did not have far to travel and there was nothing to be lost in running him. Favourite was Durius who, trained by Staff Ingham, had brought off a gamble in a selling race at Hurst Park, for which there was no penalty, and was ridden by an apprentice claiming an allowance. Consequently Cloud of Glory, who was penalised for winning at Newbury and had no weight allowance, was set to give Durius 10lbs. Again Cloud of Glory ran a fine race, taking the lead at half way and only losing it inside the final furlong, going under to Durius by a length. So impressed was Staff by this performance that he offered us £4,000 for Cloud of Glory, subject to the usual veterinary examination. We agreed to this, but found he was rather jarred after the race, so had to defer the examination. It was two or three weeks before he was fit to be galloped for his wind and when this was done he was found to make a noise. Consequently the deal fell through. Cloud of Glory ran again three more times without success and was sold cheaply to Peter Thrale, a trainer for whom I sometimes rode and who passed him on to go pony racing. The last I heard of him was reading that he had finished second in the Pony Derby at Hawthorn Hill.

Tony had a brief association with another horse before retiring from the Turf. This was a gelding I bought privately from Ted Martindale, who had been in the professional polo world and, now an old man, used to buy cheap yearlings at the sales and resell them later. He was an extremely good judge who bought entirely on conformation, and always was to be seen at the entrance to the sale ring, where he could get a close look at the lots before they went in to be sold. He wore an old leather coat, was rather bent and lame, doubtless from falls from horses, and carried a shooting stick to give himself a periodic rest. Ted lived near Rugby and kept his horses with a neighbouring farmer friend, Mr. Dobson I think was his name, who as much to befriend Ted and give him an interest, took a share in them and fed them. I bought several horses from Ted, all winning if not in England, abroad. A characteristic I remember particularly about him was that he had beautiful handwriting, similar to that of Miss F.M. Prior, the distinguished Turf historian and a successful owner breeder on a modest scale, about her last good horse being Runnymede, an attractive little grey colt by Petition out of Dutch Clover by Winterhalter, trained by Bill Wightman at Bishops Waltham. Runnymede was a useful sprinter, winning the Berkshire Stakes and Palace House Stakes (Group III) among other races and doing quite well as a sire below the top class, his best winners probably being The Go-Between (Cornwallis Stakes) and Streak (National Stakes). Miss Prior was a scholarly lady with a fine knowledge of pedigrees and Turf lore, on which she wrote several highly regarded books. She had firm ideas on economy and left Bill Wightman, despite a number of successful years with him, because he raised his fees from £12 a week to £12.10s. After departing the stable she never won another race.

Returning to our purchase from Ted Martindale, this was a well-made bay gelding, then two years old, just under 16 hands, with excellent limbs, in build strong, lengthy and workmanlike. He was a little lacking in quality, but made up for it in an honest, kind head, with a big eye and slightly lop ears. He was by Pink Flower out of Idle Jest, by Flamboyant and was bred by King George VI. His sire Pink Flower had an interesting pedigree as he was by the great German horse Oleander, out of Plymstock, dam of The Oaks winner Pennycomequick. We decided to call the gelding Tickled Pink, and when applying for this name discovered that he already had one, Pink Jester. However, since he had not raced we

114

were able to change the name to Tickled Pink, which we preferred. He went to be trained by Tom Masson and raced five times, three times at two and twice at three, but proved terribly backward and, since his last three races were selling races, I decided that it was a waste of money to keep him in training and that we should turn him out at a farm which Tony owned, and try to sell him as a prospective jumper. We did so, but were unable to find a buyer at even a modest price. One day Jean, who thought that Tickled Pink should not be disposed of for a pittance, said that she would give us £50 for him and get George Todd, with whom she had a successful partnership in Holy Deadlock, to go halves, he paying nothing but training him free. Tony agreed – and got the £50 – and the horse, by now four, went to George Todd.

At Manton Tickled Pink began to improve and was suited to the long distance work which George Todd gave him. He was at the bottom of the handicap, and on his first appearance from his new stable finished fourth in a moderate handicap over one-and-a-half miles at Bath. Next he ran third in a mile-and-a-half selling handicap, again at Bath, won an apprentice handicap over the same distance, at Ascot, and ended the season by finishing fifth in a two-mile handicap at Lingfield. From then on he continued to show gradual improvement, and the following year, after running twice unplaced and second twice, once in a seller and once in a handicap, I was allowed on him for his final appearance of the season in an amateur's race at Windsor, which he won. Tickled Pink raced until he was seven, when he was at his best. He could have continued, but unfortunately was struck by an internal inflammation and had to be put down. While at Manton Tickled Pink ran 24 times, won eight races, including the Carnarvon Cup at Salisbury twice and the Kilkerran Cup at Ayr twice, finished second four times, including in the Goodwood Stakes as a seven-year-old, and was third once. He carried me in six races and won all of them, was a delightful ride, willing to make running or wait, went on any going and was as courageous as he was kind. It was a sad day for us all when he had to be put down.

10

CONTEMPORARY 'BUMPERS'

Of those of my contemporaries among amateur riders who survived the war and continued to ride during the decade after it, Anthony Mildmay, Bobby Petre, Tubby Parker, Dick Black and Reg Tweedie were the leaders under N.H. Rules. Anthony Mildmay, Lord Mildmay of Flete as he was then, through enthusiasm, dedication and generous patronage of the sport in the shape of the number of horses he owned, was top of the list. He was a brave, strong and competent rider, able to stand up to the physical hardships of the game, a sound tactician and a great asset to N.H. racing. Popular in and out of the jockeys' room, he really understood what jumping was about, from a thoroughly professional angle. It was a tragedy when he was drowned bathing in the sea.

Tall and handicapped by a neck injury, which troubled him from time to time, he was not so stylish as Bobby Petre or Tubby Parker and seldom rode on the flat, but was most effective over jumps. Anthony, who was godfather to our elder son Ian, was a delightful character, who blended a realisation of the responsibilities of his position with a warm understanding of human nature and people in all walks of life. The professionals respected and trusted him. "Go on Milord, this one isn't fancied," a jockey shouted at him when finding himself going better than was convenient during a race. Anthony appreciated his predicament, sent his horse on and made no comment on the somewhat injudicious exhortation. Anthony seemed unlucky to lose the National of 1948, in which he finished third to Sheila's Cottage and First of the Dandies, riding his own horse Cromwell. During the last stages of the race his neck went out of place, causing his head to sink on his chest, severely handicapping him. It was thought that the same trouble caused his death from drowning. In the 'National of 1936, Anthony was unluckier still: with the race apparently at his mercy, the buckle of his reins came undone and his mount Davy Jones ran out. In the immediate post-war years, "Come on Milord" became as familiar a cry from the stands at jumping meetings as was "Come on Steve", in relation to Steve Donoghue on the flat in earlier times.

Bobby Petre was a fine rider, particularly over fences; he later turned professional, but soon afterwards lost his leg as a result of an unbelievable accident. He was then training, and during a spell of hard weather had taken his horses to work on the beach. He was standing on a low breakwater and in stepping down landed awkwardly, breaking his leg so badly that it had to be amputated. A man of ebullient nature and remarkable fortitude, he met this disaster with superb equanimity, was soon riding about again and has never let this setback interfere with his life. Dick Black, whom I had known since we were boys hunting with the Dumfriesshire, was another who turned professional and more than held his own in that milieu. He was a strong, effective rider, better over obstacles than on the flat and as an amateur won the Cheltenham Gold Cup on Fortina, owned by the late Lord Grimthorpe and trained by Hector Christie. Fortina was a French-bred entire, a chestnut of beautiful quality, who became an outstanding sire of jumpers. Tubby Parker was a top-class all rounder, stylish, competent and tough. He farmed in Norfolk and I first met him before the War riding at those delightful meetings Fakenham, Hethersett and Bungay, of which only the first remains. He always had a horse or two of his own, which raced under the distinctive 'grey, orange cap', the reverse of the more famous colours of Marcel Boussac. Tubby later came into the news as the breeder of the 1971 'National winner Specify. Reg Tweedie the champion amateur of the north was as good an all-rounder as you would find and particularly effective over fences. Most of his riding took place in the north, but he was a formidable opponent when he came south for the N.H. meeting at Cheltenham and on other occasions. Reg and his wife bred some good horses, notably Freddie, who twice finished second in the National, to Jay Trump in 1965 and to Anglo the following year. Unfortunately Reg had given up race riding by then, for they would have made a fine partnership. However, he had a lot of fun hunting Freddie, who is reputed to have jumped several five-barred gates out hunting the week before contesting one of his 'Nationals. The Tweedies also bred some good flat racers out of their mare Rosie Wings, whose sire Telegram II was a good hurdler for Miss Dorothy Paget. The best of the progeny of

Rosy Wings were Mount Athos (Sunny Way), who finished third to Sir Ivor and Connaught in The Derby of 1968, and John Splendid (Sing Sing), a good sprinter whose victories included the Ayr Gold Cup, an appropriate success since Reg, by this time a member of the Jockey Club, as is Sandy Struthers, who owned John Splendid, and the horse's trainer, John Dunlop, are all Scotsmen.

The three best amateurs against whom I rode before the war, Alec Marsh, Perry Harding and the American, Pete Bostwick, had all retired from the English race riding scene by the end of the war. Alec became a starter, eventually reaching the top in this branch as Jockey Club starter. Perry, who had a distinguished war record and rose to the rank of General, hung up his boots after a winning ride abroad when still in the Army. Pete Bostwick took up training in America where he also rode several winners at a veteran age for a jockey, and was active to his death a few years ago. On the flat Gerald Armstrong, one of the few amateurs to ride 100 winners under this code, had more or less retired before the war, but returned to ride a winner before giving up for good. Teddy Underdown, with whom I had dead-heated for top amateur on the flat in 1939, was still going. Frank Cundell, an outstanding amateur under both Rules, had given up riding over jumps, continuing for a season or so after the war on the flat, before concentrating on training. Frank, who qualified and practised as a vet, knew the racing game through and through. Apart from his skill as a rider, he was a fine judge of a horse and a first-class trainer, both of flat racers and jumpers. Later he proved an invaluable addition to the official side of racing as a steward.

One of Frank's former owners paid him a warm tribute: "You couldn't find a nicer chap to train with. He got the absolute best out of his horses, placed them brilliantly, always rang you up to discuss when and where they were going to run and, if you weren't at the meeting, telephoned you to tell you exactly what had happened." His horses invariably looked beautiful and were immaculately turned out; he was a real professional. Frank trained a remarkable horse, Crudwell, who won 50 races out of 108 starts, flat, fences and hurdles, including the Welsh Grand National. Crudwell was a beautifully balanced, well-made, good-looking gelding, appropriately by Noble Star, because this horse had been trained by Frank's father, Len, to win the Ascot Stakes, Cesarewitch and Jockey Club Cup. Noble Star was the last sire of note in England to come from the St. Simon male line, before it was revived by the importation of Bois Roussel and Prince Chevalier. Frank died in 1983.

Among the other pre-war amateurs still riding were Ronnie Strutt (now Lord Belper), who gave me a good ride in the National before the war on his own horse, Sporting Piper – I think he was out of action from a fall – and Ginger Dennistoun, a prolific rider of winners over fences before the war; both rode only on the flat after the war. Ginger had been in 5 Company at Sandhurst with me and, though only a term senior, was riding winners several years before I had any success. Ginger was a strong and competent rider on the flat, if not particularly stylish, and rode a number of winners after the war before giving up to train, when he put me on a winner on the flat. Ginger twice trained the winner of the Imperial Cup with High Point. Some years later, when I had given up race riding and had started hunting again, I was talking to Ginger and asked him if he ever went out hunting. Since he had been a fearless rider over fences in his youth, I was surprised when he replied: "Hunting! The other day I got on the quietest horse in my yard – the first time I'd been on a horse for ages – and hadn't gone ten yards before I was so terrified that I had to get off." Bob Colling used to say: "You never lose your nerve, you only get more cunning," but age does not affect every-one the same way. Latterly Ginger took to yachting and on one occasion his boat was moored beside another, upon which a late-night, noisy party was taking place, greatly to his annoyance. After several attempts to quieten the party had failed, Ginger – expressing himself colourfully and with vigour, and doubtless having imbibed generously as a panacea to the din – decided to complain to the police. He drove to the police station and, finding his complaint received disinterestedly, he launched a robust verbal attack on the officer in charge, which ended by Ginger getting locked up himself. Sadly, Ginger was killed in a car accident through no fault of his own.

A colourful and eccentric pre-war amateur rider, who rode again after the war, was Derek Jackson. One of the most distinguished scientists of his day, his subject being spectroscopy, he did invaluable work in this sphere in the 1939–45 war, insisting on joining the RAF and flying operationally to test his theories in practice and winning the DFC and AFC. There is an excellent and entertaining portrait of Derek in Diana Mosley's book 'Life of Contrast'. Diana knew Derek well, as he was married at one time to her sister Pam, and recalls the occasion when a high-up officer in the Air Force, whom Derek had addressed as an equal, remarked to him: "We have a tradition in the Royal Air Force, when a very junior officer addresses a very senior officer he calls him Sir." To this Derek replied: "Oh do you? In racing it's quite different, the profes-sionals call the amateurs Sir!" Complete disregard for authority or rank was always a feature of Derek's character, evident on the Turf as elsewhere. On one occasion at Wye, where racing ceased many years ago, Derek complained to the Stewards about the insanitary state of the jockeys' lavatories, which were earth closets. The Stewards informed him that they had inspected them and that in their opinion they were perfectly satisfactory. The rejoinder to this was: "It's all very well inspecting them, you try shitting in them." This earned him a fine of £10 and a rebuke for impertinence, whereupon he produced his cheque book and said: "I'll make the cheque out for £12 and then you can split it up between the three of you." As a rider, Derek was fearless, if some way short of professional standard. He was old for steeplechasing and, on account of his scientific work and social life, not always entirely fit. As a result he was sometimes unable to do full justice to his mounts. Once, when asked by the Stewards why he had pulled up one of his horses, which appeared full of running, he replied, "Because I got tired," adding some unflattering observations on the equitational ability of his inquisitors and their probable actions in similar circumstances.

Later after giving up riding, Derek moved to Paris and continued with his scientific work. He bred and raced horses in France, on the flat, with considerable success; among his winners was Yami, one of the best three-year-old fillies of her year. At that time Derek was a major shareholder in the News of the World, and through him I went to work for the paper as racing correspondent until, as a result of Derek wishing to sell his shares, the paper was bought by Rupert Murdoch and I resigned. Jean and I saw quite a bit of Derek when we went racing in France, and I spoke to him regularly on the telephone during his final illness, when he had to have a foot amputated. He was one of the most amusing, unusual and certainly one of the most academically talented riders the Turf has ever known.

Jakie Astor, who before the war rode under both Rules, now kept to the flat and rode a number of winners. He still had some jumpers in training, mostly with Nat Smyth, but one named Goer was with Tom Masson. Goer won a hurdle race at Windsor, ridden by Matt Feakes, a professional who, I believe, once had the unusual distinction of riding the winner of a hunters' 'chase because the conditions of the race omitted the customary clause confining it to amateur riders. Goer won the race after surviving an objection. In those days there was no patrol camera and the evidence of jockeys carried considerable weight with the Stewards in deciding objections: and when we were all having a drink afterwards Matt Feakes remarked to Jakie: "I don't know if I did right, governor, but I heard the rider of the second offer the one on the third a fiver to speak up for him, so I offered him a tenner."

Soon a new generation of amateurs began to appear, some good ones among them, a number of whom later turned professional. One was Dick Francis, now world-famous as a thriller writer, who headed the N.H. list as a professional and surely was the unluckiest man ever to lose a 'National, when Devon Loch slid on to his belly on the run-in with the race won. The reason for this has never been solved. Other successful amateurs later to turn professional were Michael Scudamore, who won the 'National on Oxo and is father of the professional champion N.H. rider, Peter; Atty Corbet, who had a distinguished war record, became a successful trainer and was killed while walking with his string when he was run down by a car, the driver of which was blinded by the sun. One of the owners for whom Atty used to ride was Baron Hatvany, an odd-looking gentleman – something between Svengali and the Hunchback of Notre Dame – with a very good-looking wife. Of him Atty once observed, "When you win he's a Hungarian nobleman, when you lose he's a Central European Yid." Alan Oughton, who afterwards trained, but tragically died prematurely from cancer; David Punshom, later a stipendiary steward abroad. Those who remained amateurs included the two farmers Joe Spencer and Danny Moralee, the latter an exceptionally good rider; the brothers John and Clive Straker; John Eustace-Smith, alas, killed in a steeplechase; John Bosley, now a successful trainer, whose son Martin is doing well as a N.H. professional; John Cousins from Cheshire; Gay Kindersley and Bob McCreery, who both headed the amateurs' list. All were talented riders under both Rules, with whom I had a lot of fun, mostly on the flat, as my post-war career under N.H. rules was a brief one. Gay was so named before the word came into general use as indicating homosexuality; and on one occasion at a public function, forgetting this interpretation he went up with a fellow guest to a stranger, who was looking rather lost, and somewhat nonplussed him by saying, "I'm Gay and this is my friend." John Ciechanowski rode mostly in France, becoming European champion.

An eminent amateur on the flat, who rode in France and England, was Prince Aly Khan. I knew him from pre-war years, when he rode in England regularly with considerable success, and had kindly given me my first ride in France. This was on an attractive grey horse named Faithful, who finished second. Faithful was said to have been commandeered as a charger by a German general when France was overrun in the war. Aly was popular in racing circles and society – except with cuckolded husbands whose wives found him irresistible. Strikingly good-looking, vivacious and amusing, Aly was a true enthusiast. Until his father, the late Aga Khan, stopped him, he hunted in England and rode in point-to-points. He served in the Middle East during the war, riding a winner or two in Cairo when on leave. He liked to make the running in a race and was a good judge of pace, a modest winner and a good loser. On his reappearance in England as a rider after the war, at Salisbury, he was greeted with enthusiasm by all who had known him in pre-war days, Jakie Astor remarking: "Hello, Al, it's good to see you again. I thought you'd given up the saddle for the couch." Aly was a good judge of a horse and loved a deal, one of his most notable trans- actions being to arrange the sale of the subsequent Derby winner, Bois Roussel. Concerning this deal, which at the time looked a by no means favourable purchase on Peter Beatty's part, someone remarked: "I think it's disgraceful the way Aly stuffed that Derby winner into Peter Beatty." Breeding did not have the same attraction for Aly as it has for the present Aga, Karim, who is more knowledgeable about it and has a more serious and scientific approach. Aly was an inveterate gambler, both on horses and at the tables, which was his chief weakness. He was a generous and agreeable host, as Jean and I found when staying with him at Deauville. It was a free and easy household at the Villa Goriza – usually referred to as the Villa Gorilla – the only stipulation being that guests dined in, changed, and were punctual. "If you ever want a bed, always let me know; if the worst comes to the worst, you can always sleep in a bathroom," he once told me. Aly's death in a motor accident was a tragedy, leaving many saddened at his loss.

Among the good amateurs who later turned professional was Reg Hollinshead, now training successfully under both Rules. He still recalls a race at Lincoln, on the flat, which ended more happily for him than for me. It was at the stage of my riding career when, through other commit- ments, I was finding it difficult to keep fit. Though having no weight problems I needed a great deal of work – to use a training term – to keep in proper racing condition. At that time there were few amateur races on the flat, I had given up riding jumping, and though I exercised vigor- ously in other ways, it was an unsatisfactory substitute for the real thing. On this occasion I was riding a mare called Safety Light, blinkered for the first time, who was pulling my arms out. By the time we turned for home I was dead-beat, she dropped her bit and appeared to have lost all interest in the race. Meanwhile, Reg Hollinshead had shot into a ten- length lead and had the race won. Unfortunately he started to pull up as the winning post approached and the gap lessened but, seeing no hope of winning and being exhausted, I made no effort to rally my horse. It must have looked bad, as I was had up before the Stewards to explain my riding. Lord Hothfield and Colonel 'Squeak' Thompson were two of the Stewards, both of whom I knew. The latter, who had a sharp sense of humour and had been a good amateur rider in his day, was asking me the most awkward questions he could devise and getting considerable entertainment at my difficulty in answering them, as I had no wish to plead unfitness. At one stage matters seemed to be going so badly for me that it looked as if I was due for a visit to Cavendish Square, where the offices of the Jockey Club then were. Eventually I was let off the hook as a result of the mare wearing blinkers for the first time, and given a rebuke for not making more effort, though that would have been to no avail.

Not long after my depressing experience when beaten on Safety Light, Stanley Wootton asked me to ride a horse called Hutchin – named after his gamekeeper – at Windsor. This was an honour, since Stanley almost never ran horses in amateur races. The greatest maker of jockeys in Turf history, his 'cerise, gold sleeves, pale blue cap', were almost invariably worn by past or present pupils. I was only too pleased to accept, but a little apprehensive about doing justice to the horse, whom I had never seen, let alone ridden. The race was a mile-and-a-half handicap at Windsor on November 7th, 1952 and there were ten runners, including Safety Light, this time ridden by Ronnie Belper. It was a beautiful still November day, with the autumn leaves still on the trees round the paddock. Stanley Wootton was at Liverpool and had sent Jack Sirett, a retired former Wootton pupil and jockey, in charge of Hutchin. As soon as I saw the horse, I was entranced by him. He was a beautiful little brown gelding, round as an apple and bright as a button, with an attractive, masculine head and a kind intelligent expression. Though his coat had broken, it carried the glow of health and his well-being was evident in his periodically jumping and kicking, squealing with delight. I knew we would get on. My instructions were to wait with him, go the shortest way and produce him inside the last furlong. Favourite at 11–4 was Daytime, who had been backed down from 4–1; he had won his last two races and appeared to have much the best form. Hutchin, who drifted from 7–2 to 5–1 was joint second favourite with Border Cross, ridden by Sir Gordon Richard's son Peter, who afterwards trained for E.P. Taylor in Canada and now runs a stud there. Everything came my way. Two furlongs out, there were five horses abreast in front of me, all bumping each other. Safety Light came out best, taking the lead on the rails. A convenient gap appeared on her near side inside the last furlong, enabling Hutchin to come through to win by a length. Few victories pleased me more, capped by Jack Sirett commenting: "The Governor couldn't have ridden him better himself."

In the year of my retirement a notable amateur appeared on the scene, John Lawrence, now Lord Oaksey. He had no rides on the flat that season, so we never met in a race. John went on to a distinguished riding career, chiefly over fences and hurdles, being twice leading N.H. amateur, finishing second in the Grand National on Carrickbeg in 1963, and in 1958 achieving the remarkable double for an amateur of riding the winners of the Imperial Cup and Whitbread Gold Cup. He has since gained comparable repute as a journalist and TV personality.

11

RIDES FOR OTHER TRAINERS

Apart from the trainers already mentioned were a number of pre-war friends who gave me rides when peace returned. Gordon Johnson-Houghton, father of the trainer, Fulke, was one. Gordon and I were at Newmarket together in the 1930s, he with Jack Colling, I with Victor Gilpin, when I had some happy days staying at his home in Cheshire for Liverpool races, as related in *Far from a Gentleman* (the first volume of my memoirs). After the war Gordon set up training at Blewbury with success. He was one of the first to realise that horses could be bought reasonably in France and exploited in England, putting this to good advantage with such as Laurentis, Le Lavandou, Periscope III and Fast Soap, on whom he gave me a winning ride and who won the City and Suburban Handicap at Epsom, at that time a race of importance. One of Gordon's chief patrons was Miss Dorothy Paget, whose Silver Gate, a beautiful grey entire by The Phoenix, was another winner trained by him which I rode. A true eccentric, Dorothy Paget spent a fortune on her racing, winning a war-time Derby with Straight Deal (Solario-Good Deal, by Appelle), also the Grand National and five Cheltenham Gold Cups with Golden Miller, one of the greatest 'chasers of all time, and four Champion Hurdles, two with Insurance, the others with Solford and Distel. As a young woman Miss Paget had been a good rider, winning in the show ring and a point-to-point, but later put on weight and took no trouble with her looks. Unkempt in dress, she wore the same overcoat year after year because she thought it lucky. She stayed up to all hours, a chef being employed night and day to cope with her voracious appetite, due probably to a medical condition. On the racecourse she was liable to keep the catering and cloakroom staff on duty long after the last race, tipping them generously in return. For years her chief trainer on the flat was Walter Nightingall, with whom she eventually quarrelled, most of the horses going to Gordon Houghton, with whom they remained until Gordon was killed in a hunting accident in 1952. Her famous disagreement with her jumping trainer Basil Briscoe over Golden Miller's failure in the National in which Gerry Wilson was dislodged is history. The jumpers went to Owen Anthony and later Fulke Walwyn, who won her a Cheltenham Gold Cup with Mont Tremblant. The one person with whom Dorothy Paget never quarrelled was Charlie Rogers, manager of her Ballymacoll Stud in Ireland which on her death was bought by the late Sir Michael Sobell. She always referred to him as Romeo, and besides his professional expertise, Charlie knew how to deal with her whims and foibles.

I carried Miss Paget's 'blue, yellow hoop on body and sleeves, yellow cap with blue hoops' to win on Silver Gate and Kinsale, also trained by Gordon Johnson-Houghton. On the second occasion the owner was present. A favourite ploy of Miss Paget was to have two or more horses running the same day, which she would back in doubles and accumulators; this was one. That day her first runner, Explorer, trained by Charlie Forester and ridden by Tommy Gosling, had been beaten in the previous race. When I entered the parade-ring and was introduced to her, she at once addressed me: "I hope you're going to win for us, Mr. Hislop, and get me out of trouble. Did you see the last race? My jockey rode a dreadful race on my horse, he should have won." Tactfully and truthfully I replied that I had not seen the race as I was in the jockeys' room getting ready, but hoped that we would win. As usual, she was wearing her old, blue-grey woollen coat – it was worn regardless of the temperature – and was covered in lucky charms of various sorts. She was in a highly excitable state, chain-smoking and making periodical, derogatory references to the unfortunate Gosling's efforts in the previous event. When the 'jockeys up' signal was given, the lad leading Kinsale brought the horse towards us, whereupon Miss Paget barked out: "Don't bring him here, we were unlucky when the horse came here in the last race. Take him to the other end of the ring." This was done, Gordon legged me up, Miss Paget wished me good luck, adding, "and mind you win!" Since Kinsale had a great deal in hand he won easily, which was just as well for me, and Miss Paget was delighted.

Two other friends for whom I was lucky enough to have winning rides were the late John de Moraville and Neville Crump, the latter happily well and recently retired. Both had similar backgrounds in that they were originally in the cavalry before mechanisation, and were fine horse-masters; their horses always looked superb. They were also extremely good trainers; Neville Crump sent out the National winners, Sheila's Cottage, Teal and Merryman II, and John de Moraville's many successes from a small string included the Queen Alexandra Stakes at Royal Ascot with Vulgan, who was also a good hurdler and went on to become an outstanding sire of jumpers. John also trained one of the best two-mile 'chasers of the day, a truly magnificent French-bred entire, nearly black, called Rondo II. He was a big, strong individual, full of quality and difficult to fault. Before Rondo II went 'chasing John asked me to ride him in a hurdle race at Manchester; I was thrilled at the idea, as he was my ideal of a jumper and he looked a certainty, but Jean reminded me that we had promised to go to stay with John and Jane Nelson (Major-General Sir John and Lady Jane Nelson), near Cheltenham, for a race meeting there. Both John and Jane are old friends from pre-war days. John, who had a most distinguished war record and I first met in 1930 when we went for an interview with the 14th/20th Hussars – neither of us ended up there. We saw a good bit of each other when John was at Cambridge and I at Newmarket, and Jane, then unmarried, was living at Euston, the seat of the Dukes of Grafton not far from Newmarket. In pre-marital days, nothing – no social engagement or most inviting of assignations – would have stood in the way of such a ride; but I was prevailed upon to refuse, the ride going to Jack Moloney, a great jockey then verging on retirement, who had an easy victory on Rondo II. It did Jack a good turn, as he was having few rides and needed any money he could get; but I was deeply disappointed since I so admired the horse. To cap it all, we never got to stay with the Nelsons in the end, I think through lack of petrol, which then was still rationed.

Another pre-war friend was the late Dick Warden, of whom I have written in *Far From a Gentleman* and *Anything but a Soldier*. He had emerged from the war a Lieutenant-Colonel, having served in a hazardous capacity in occupied France, and trained at Newmarket for Peter Fitzwilliam (Earl Fitzwilliam), a war-time Commando, who was killed after the war in a flying accident. For them I had a couple of winning rides on a beautiful, big, strong colt by Signal Light called Liberty Light. Though Dick had always been in racing, fox-hunting was the sport dearest to him, and at one time he was Master of the Ledbury Hounds. When at Harrow he was allowed to hunt with the Pinner Drag Hounds on Saturdays, instead of playing football. Once, when there was a particularly good line laid on a Wednesday, of which Dick wanted to take advantage, he applied for leave to go to the dentist that afternoon, which his housemaster granted. As he crept down the stairs, kitted out in boots, breeches, tweed jacket and bowler hat, and armed with a cutting whip, he came face to face with his housemaster, who remarked: "Ah, Warden, going to the dentist, I believe, and, if I may say so, most appropriately attired," never referring to the matter again. After training for a few years, Dick joined the Curragh Bloodstock Agency. He was largely instrumental in introducing Sheikh Mohammed to English racing, buying much of the bloodstock which brought him such success. Dick then retired to concentrate on his own horses, which carried the 'jade-green, flame hooped sleeves, black cap' to victories under both Rules, until he died in 1990.

An old friend from my days at Newmarket in the 1930s was Bob Colling who, though born in 1872, was still training at Bedford Lodge in the Bury Road and gave me a winning ride after the war. Originally apprenticed to William l'Anson, whose daughter he married, Bob was the father of the trainers Jack and George, both good jockeys on the flat before becoming successful trainers. Bob himself was a competent flat race jockey before getting too heavy, and had the odd ride over fences and hurdles: he told me that he never left the ground in the first hurdle race in which he took part, all the panels in front of him having been knocked down; also, that he won a steeplechase on a horse which had never jumped a steeplechase fence before, and he stipulated that he rode it in a double bridle. Bob rode in the days when the modern racing seat was unheard of; he was a fine horseman, able to cope with any difficult horse in his string at an age when most of his contemporaries had forsaken the saddle. He had a robust and light-hearted view of racing and life in general, one of his observations being, "ninety percent of colts should be cut, and all the jockeys." Bob's first love was foxhunting, and he once told me that he wished that he had taken up hunting as a profession, instead of going into racing. He was a first-class man to hounds, never in a hurry, always going the shortest way but never jumping an unnecessary fence and riding to hunt as opposed to hunting to ride. Concerning this philosophy he used to delight in telling a story about the late John Johnstone of Hallheaths in Dumfriesshire, a successful amateur rider and a hard man to go out hunting, but inclined to show off by pulling out and conspicuously jumping a big place, not always when this was necessary. One day John Johnstone and Bob Colling were in a hunt with the Zetland, riding behind the huntsman, John Johnstone on a horse called Searchlight, which had won the high-jump at the

International Horse Show at Olympia. The huntsman was going through a gate and, seeing who was behind him, called out: "Just a minute Mr. Johnstone, and I'll shut it so you can jump it." This and some of the many stories about Bob Colling are repeated in *Far From a Gentleman*. The horse on which he gave me the winning ride was Manar, a strong, well-made gelding by Colombo, the race a 10-furlong handicap at Leicester. His owner was a gentleman who made motorboats, of whom Bob observed: "A nice fellow, but can't understand why horses don't perform like his boats and always run dead consistently." Manar raced best on soft ground, which he found when winning with me at Leicester; but the next time I rode him, at Sandown, the going was firm and he was beaten into second place. The winner was Victory Salute, ridden by David Punshon and trained at Epsom by Jack Reardon. When I congratulated Jack after the race he smiled rather wryly, and said: "As a matter of fact I didn't fancy him. He pulls rather hard and has to be waited with, so I put a rubber bit on him, thinking that Punshon wouldn't hold him, but it didn't work out that way." Jack, whose ways were, to say the least, devious, doubtless did not want his jockey to think that the horse was unfancied. But Pushon, who was attached to the stable, may have smelt a rat and, knowing the horse, have covered him up so that he had to come from behind; or Victory Salute might just have felt that way himself. Had Jack's subterfuge succeeded, Manar would have won in spite of the firm ground.

Towards the end of my riding career amateur races on the flat had begun to dwindle, but due largely to the efforts of Gay Kindersley, the first Secretary of the Amateur Riders Association of Great Britain, of which he is now President, the position began to improve. Now, greatly helped by the international association, FEGENTRI, and the scope for lady riders, amateur racing under both Rules flourishes. This is as it should be. The amateur has always been an integral part of racing, giving practical experience and understanding of the sport to the officials of the future, providing a stepping stone for aspiring professionals and bringing into the game as owners people who otherwise might never have entered it.

12

JOURNALISM

I had a bit of money from investments, but not enough to be able to get by without a job. During the war Jakie Astor, in whose Phantom Squadron I was serving, asked me what I was going to do after the war. I said that I thought of trying to become a racing journalist, as it would be possible to combine this with race riding. When invalided out of the Army for a period, as a result of a fall in a steeplechase, I wrote one or two pieces for *Men Only* on racing, which were well received. It was pleasant work and seemed the most suitable milieu. Jakie replied that he thought that his brother David, who owned *The Observer*, might be looking for a racing correspondent, and that he would mention me to him. This pleased me, since a Sunday paper offered more freedom than a daily one, leaving scope for other activities. The conversation took place towards the end of the war and, being older than Jakie, I was demobilised first, in 1945. The following year I had a message from David Astor, inviting me to come to see him with a view to working for *The Observer*. The outcome was that a trial article should be submitted and, if this proved acceptable, he would take me on as racing correspondent. All went well and I began sixteen happy years with the paper. The editor then was Ivor Brown, later to be succeeded by David Astor himself. The former was a pleasant, amiable teddy-bear of a man, a couple of whose books on words I had found helpful to my previous writing efforts. Uninterested in racing, he gave me a free hand to write what I pleased. Likewise the sports editor, Harold Gale, a newspaperman through and through and a real professional, whose only instruction to me, delivered once a year, was: "I always think that during the winter it's a good plan to review the future prospects of the past season's leading two-year-olds." Reputed to have drunk a bottle of whisky a day which, even if true, had no discernable effect, Harold Gale had only a cursory knowledge of racing, but told me that once, when out of work and hard up, he decided to try his luck as a tipster. He advertised in the sporting press under a pseudonym, received a number of replies and sent out tips selected more or less with a pin. By some stroke of luck he had a successful run and the money flowed in, but inevitably his fortune changed and after a series of losers he had to close down, though a few loyal supporters wrote asking if he was going to start up again. Eventually Harold Gale retired and was succeeded by a series of sports editors, the best of these being Michael Davie, who later rose to the top of his profession where he remains.

The only sports editor with whom I did not get on was Chris Brasher, who had won an Olympic Gold Medal in the steeplechase. He was an able feature writer, but not easy to work for, as he knew nothing about racing, though by no means convinced of this, and tried to impose an aggressive policy for the sake of aggression, which I disliked and refused to follow. Alan Ross, a poet of merit and a fine writer, who contributed the article on cricket, felt the same and told me that unless Brasher was removed he would resign. We cannot have been alone in our reactions, as Brasher's tenure as sports editor was brief and he was removed to areas more suited to his nature and ability.

In those days racing correspondents had more space than now, at least a thousand words, some papers carrying two such articles. Style was more leisured and elaborate, and the racing press had one or two relics from a past age, whose columns were littered with cliches, heavy sentences and Latinised words which were the fashion of their youth. These writers, however, knew more about horses and racing history than the average, modern racing journalist, having been brought up in a pre-motorised environment, ridden from childhood, often hunted and perhaps ridden racing as amateurs. The older racing journalists I remember best were Meyrick Good and Sam Long, both of *The Sporting Life*. Meyrick had hunted and ridden on the flat as an amateur, Sam Long came from a farming background, and recalled riding over to see Alec Taylor at Manton as a boy. He asked Alec Taylor if he had ever had a bet, to which the reply was "No". Then, "I'm wrong; I did once have a bet, I had £25 on Sceptre in the Jockey Club Cup. I galloped her with some good horses and thought that if she could finish upsides them she was a certainty. She beat them in a canter." Needless to say, Sceptre won the Jockey Club Cup. Meyrick Good had an excellent knowledge of racing and horses and was a sound judge of running, but his prose would not have pleased purists. He seldom gave racecourses their ordinary names: Sandown would be 'the Surrey slopes', Alexandra Park 'the Wood Green venue'; owners whose hospitality he had savoured became 'best of sportsmen and most genial of hosts', while jockeys were often termed 'knights of the pigskin'. Not that cliches and superfluous phrases are unknown today; jockeys 'riding like men possessed' and flushes of double adjectives sometimes appear even in the racing columns of the 'heavies'. One of the outstanding professionals to follow those of the era of Meyrick Good and Sam Long was James Park of the *Evening Standard*, whose assistant was Richard Baerlein, who now writes for *The Observer* and *The Guardian*. Park, a Scotsman, did not have a racing background – I believe he emanated from the world of athletics – but through hard work, intelligence and discerning observation he learnt every aspect, not least horses' conformation and fitness. He was an excellent judge of form and running, giving his readers many winners. His copy contained no frills, being direct, economic and to the point; nor, as Richard Baerlein found, was Park backward with criticism.

Sports editors often included former Oxford or Cambridge Blues; and following an age in which it was neither necessary nor fashionable for many young men to earn a living, several of these later became racing journalists. Nor were they unfitted to the task. Having been interested in the sport from their earliest days, they were able on leaving school to devote themselves to racing and betting. While some fell by the wayside trying to defeat the bookmakers, those who survived gleaned much from the experience. After the war, with this experience behind them, being reasonably well-educated and dedicated to the Turf, a number of them entered racing journalism and improved the general literary standard of this branch of the profession. They included a strong coterie of old Etonians. Most senior were the Gilbey brothers, Geoffrey and Quinny, who in their time wrote for a varied selection of papers – in 1939 Quinny was producing ten articles a week. Among the others were Richard Baerlein, Clive Graham (*Daily Express*), Bill Curling (*Daily Telegraph*), Roger Mortimer (*Sunday Times*) and Philip Clifford (*The Daily Mail*). From a comparable, if less exalted educational background, came such as Jim Snow (*The Times*), Peter O'Sullevan (*Daily Express*), Noel Carlile (*The Times*), who died early, in 1945, to be succeeded by Frank Byrne, also Peter Willett (*Sunday Times*) and I, who both had benefited from one of the great teachers of English and History, R. St. C. Talboys of Wellington. Other writers for leading papers included the senior figures, Cyril

Luckman (*Daily Express*), Eric Rickman (*Daily Mail*), who was a stickler for being addressed by his military title of Major and was succeeded by his son John, and Kenneth Bryceson (*News of the World*).

They were an agreeable coterie and I got to know most of them pretty well, though, being on a Sunday paper, more of my work was done at home than in the Press room. Possibly the best all-round writer of the lot was Clive Graham, who could deal expertly with every facet, had a photographic memory, a flair for a good story and sometimes gave an inspired long-priced winner, notably Marmaduke Jinks, a last-minute selection who won the Lincoln at 33–1. Ironically, Clive was not a lucky punter: having backed Tudor Minstrel at a long price for The Derby he declined to lay off his bet, only to see the horse beaten into fourth place, a short-priced favourite. An easy-going, attractive character, with a distinctive panache about him, Clive loved the aspect of racing immortalised by Damon Runyon and was as much at home among racecourse spivs as the aristocracy. He was also an excellent paddock commentator on TV. Clive once told me that his only dread in life was to finish a burden to those nearest to him. Sadly his wish was fulfilled only too early in life, when he died after a short illness from a tumour of the brain. Clive and Peter O'Sullevan made an outstanding team for the *Daily Express*, to whom they must have been worth a fortune. Peter's department was the gossip column, including information on French and Irish horses racing in England. He developed a unique style, which was both literary and economic, the latter an essential quality in view of the limited space at his disposal. He was extraordinarily well-informed and a good tipster, one of the reasons for his success being that, if told anything in confidence, he could be relied upon absolutely to respect it. As a result, he often acquired information not imparted to less reliable recipients. He later became the leading race reader on TV. Peter also did well as an owner with the top-class sprinter Be Friendly, later a successful sire, and the versatile little gelding Attivo, whose victories included the Triumph Hurdle and the Chester Cup. Roger Mortimer, a friend from pre-war days, had a wit combined with encyclopaedic knowledge of Turf history and an agreeably readable style. He once related to me an instance of the pitfalls of the profession when he nearly lost his job on the *Sunday Times* through writing that a horse had been 'christened' a certain name. This drew a furore of ecclesiastical wrath on him and the paper, and a severe rebuke from Lord Kemsley. Frank Byrne, who took over as chief racing writer of *The Times* after the death of Noel Carlile, had the crisp purity of style traditionally associated with this newspaper.

A tall, elegant figure, he was a good judge of racing, which was just as well since at one time he was a pretty bold punter. Perhaps as a result of his Irish background, N.H. racing was his first love, but he was as well-informed about the flat. Frank had a sharp, original wit: once when someone was quoting the advertisement for 'Phyllosan for the over-forties', Frank observed: "there's only one thing for the over-forties – prussic acid." Clive Graham's predecessor on the *Daily Express*, Cyril Luckman, was an unusual character. In appearance he somewhat resembled a benign edition of James Agate, the eminent, abrasive theatrical critic with an interest in hackney horses. Luckman seldom watched a race, but sat in the Press room writing away while it was being run; after it was over he would ask other pressmen what had happened. His work must have satisfied the exacting Lord Beaverbrook, since he held down the job for many years. One of the races which Cyril deigned to watch was The St. Leger, when he used to put on what was known as his Sidney Carton act. In those days, for The St. Leger, there was an addition to the Press stand in the form of two or three tiers of scaffolding, to afford extra viewing. Every year Cyril would put one foot on the first plank, grasp the lapel of his coat and announce: "This is a far, far better thing. . . ."

No journalist goes through his career without indignant letters from infuriated readers, and one of the most entertaining was received by a mild, inoffensive man who wrote under the name of Captain Heath. At that time there was a particularly vicious murder of a young woman, committed by a man named Neville Heath, who was hanged. Heath's journalistic namesake had just run into a spell of bad luck with his selections. This drew from a dissatisfied reader a letter which read: "so far as I'm concerned, they hanged the wrong Heath." In the tradition of the profession, there were some formidable drinkers among the racing Press. Some could demolish a bottle of gin at a sitting without detriment to their work or noticeable reaction, others were less fortunate. Jim Snow was one of the former and I can remember, one St. Leger day, seeing him with a bottle of gin in front of him, writing Kenneth Bryceson's article for him, after coping with his own, Kenneth being rather under the weather. Though able and a most pleasant character, Kenneth had a pretty casual approach to work. He had been Sports Editor to the *Daily Telegraph*, but then was on the *News of the World,* under the tolerant ownership of Sir William Carr, who rode his employees on a pretty loose rein. The crunch came when it was discovered that their racing correspondent's list of 'Twelve to Follow' contained several horses that were dead or abroad. As a result he was sacked, but the path of his departure was eased by allowing him to keep the firm's car. Frank Butler, the Sports Editor of the *News of the World*, once told me that he was called to report to Sir William Carr at St. Andrews, arriving for the meeting at 10a.m. He was greeted with, "Hello, Frank, what'll you have to drink?" Frank replied, "It's a bit early, Sir William," to which he was answered: 'I didn't ask you the time, I asked you what you wanted to drink."

Having plenty of time to work on my weekly articles, I managed to produce copy which satisfied the paper and the readers, though I found it fairly heavy weather. I was greatly helped by Jean reading through the copy before I submitted it, as she is an excellent critic and was able to point out errors of style such as repetitions. My difficulty came when an important race was on a Saturday. *The Observer* had an earlier dead-line than most papers and no access to a telephone. When the race of the day was not important there was no problem; my main article would have gone in, only two or three hundred words were needed, and the *Evening Standard* telephonist, Max Reid, obligingly would put the copy through his telephone for a small consideration. The real headache came on Grand National day. It was impossible to get my copy telephoned from the course, so I had to find a nearby householder outside the course who would let me use his telephone. I was lucky in succeeding and for several years had the kind hospitality of a family who lived about five minutes from the course. I had not yet developed the ability and confidence to dictate off the cuff, so had to get someone to telephone my copy piece by piece, which I passed to them as I wrote it. My first report on the National was particularly exacting, as I was riding in the race, in which I was third on Kami. To help me *The Observer* sent the music correspondent, the late Charles Reid. It seems an odd choice, since racing was an unknown world to him, but he could not have been a better support. He coped deftly with the copy, pointing out a flaw in phraseology here and there; the piece went through smoothly and was approved the other end. A sequel to it appeared forty-one years later, when the article was reproduced in the *Faber Book of Reportage*, edited by John Carey, which pleased me especially. In time I became proficient in telephoning my copy straight away, without first writing it down, and even earned the commendation of Chris Brasher on one of my reports of the Grand National, which needed only a single change of punctuation.

David Astor was a good editor for whom to work, approachable, helpful, critical only where this was deserved and supportive in trouble. I once involved *The Observer* in a legal matter, in which David backed me up; luckily this came to nothing. It was the result of an article, in a light vein, on an incident in South Africa. When on a visit there I went racing once or twice, finding the sport flourishing and extremely well-run, which I described. To add a touch of humour to the piece, I included a story related to me there about a colourful local racing character, whom I made identifiable by describing him as having a name that sounded like a Greek ball-game. The story was that the man in question declared an unknown apprentice to ride a horse which, in the circumstances, the public presumed was not fancied, as a result of which the horse drifted out in the betting. Shortly before the race, it was announced that the declared rider was found unfit to ride and that the leading jockey was taking his place. There was then a flood of money for the horse, shortening the price dramatically and, since the horse won, bringing off a coup. It transpired that the cause of the unfortunate apprentice's indisposition was a large dose of castor oil, timed to act shortly before the race and thus ensure his inability to ride, the leading jockey having been forewarned that he would be required. While the perpetrator took exception to the story, it was fact and not actionable; but I had also written that the man in question had been warned off, which was only partially correct since he had been warned off the chief courses, but not some of the others. There was an exchange of solicitors' letters and when the opposition realised that *The Observer* intended to ignore the matter, nothing further was heard of it.

A year or two after I joined *The Observer* I was asked to recommend someone who would write an additional article on racing. My suggestion was Jack Leach, a former successful jockey and trainer who had been writing for *The Racehorse*, a weekly publication now embodied in *The Handicap Book*. Jack had an original, entertaining style, evident in his autobiography '*Sods I have cut on the Turf*', which included one of the best descriptions of a race in his account of The Two Thousand Guineas, which he won on Adam's Apple. Jack was taken on and his work liked, but sometimes worried the Sports Editor, as he had little idea of fitting his copy to the required number of words. Accustomed from his race riding days to doing things in style, economy was a low priority with him and he shook the paper's manager, reputed to have been a former member of the Communist Party, with appropriate ideas on expenses, by flying to France first-class on a mission to report on Marcel Boussac's horses. Jack's chief fault as a writer was a tendency to live in the past: Frank Byrne once remarked of him, "He hasn't got to Manna's Derby (1925) yet." I cannot recall whether Jack drifted out of journalism or the

Grim Reaper caught up with him, but his departure was a loss, for he brought a sparkle to the business and was a likeable character.

Writing for *The Observer* was a great help, since it brought me a good deal of free-lance work with other papers; the only stipulation *The Observer* made was that I could not write for another Sunday newspaper. A further spin-off came from the BBC, to whose Sports Report programme I quite often contributed the racing part.

I was still with *The Observer* at the end of the period covered by this book, and only left the paper because David Astor most generously told me that, financially, I ought to take the greatly higher fee offered me by the *News of the World*, which *The Observer* could not match. There was a year of my contract to run, which David most kindly volunteered to waive. The chance to make the change came about through Derek Jackson, of whom I have written as a racing friend, amateur rider, eminent scientist and a most unusual character, who was a large shareholder in the *News of the World*.

At that time the policy of the *News of the World* was altering; instead of reporting the most lurid stories available and appealing chiefly to the masses, the owners decided to raise the standard, obtaining the best writers they could find and making them an offer few could afford to refuse. Thus, somewhat incongruously, in view of the paper's past reputation, it became quite an honour to write for it. Though overrunning my time as regards this book, it is perhaps pertinent to round off my regular journalistic career, which came when the *News of the World* was bought by Rupert Murdoch. I had enjoyed my spell with the paper; the work was light – though given less space I was allowed to write what I liked – the editor Stafford Somerfield, the Sports Editor Frank Butler and Stan Agate the racing editor were pleasant to work for, and the Chairman, Sir William Carr, ran the business with patriarchal understanding. An added interest was that the paper owned and raced some horses, trained by Sir Gordon Richards, and started a stud, supervised by Towser Gosden formerly a very good trainer, then retired, father of John Gosden, now sending out many good winners from Stanley House, Newmarket. The enterprise was just getting going when the newspaper was sold – ironically, because Derek Jackson wanted to realise his shares. Our winners included Tamerella, who later bred a classic winner in Germany, and Miss Print, an attractive, fast filly. We periodically met to discuss policy, after which Sir William would announce "Right, we'll go along to the canteen for some lunch", and we did so – to the Savoy Grill.

At the time of the take-over my contract was coming to an end, and I had doubts about working for the new owner. I had seen a copy of one of Murdoch's Australian papers, the quality of which made the old 'Sporting Pink' look like the Financial Times, and on my one meeting with him, I found him polite, slightly unsure of himself, bustling about in shirtsleeves and giving the impression that he had seen too many viewings of 'The Front Page'. I decided to resign, as I could see no prospect of fitting into the new regime, or of being paid the same fee, when all that would be required of the racing correspondent was tips, quotes and sensational stories. So I telephoned Stafford Somerfield and asked him to meet me for a drink. When we arrived I said, "I've got some news for you, I'm resigning." He replied, "And I've got some for you, Murdoch isn't going to renew your contract." We had a drink, parted amicably and I straightaway telephoned the Press Association to tell them that I was resigning from the News of the World as I did not wish to work for the new owner. This appeared in a number of papers and produced a furious letter from Murdoch, saying that I was no gentleman as I knew my contract was not going to be renewed, that I would cease to be employed forthwith and was to return the firm's car.

I replied, pointing out that it was I who had summoned the editor to hand in my resignation, which I did before knowing anything about my contract not being renewed, and that my contract did not cease until the end of the year, so that he was bound to it till then, adding the postscript: "Have you read Potter on gamesmanship?" To give Murdoch credit, he wrote back admitting that he was in the wrong. Whatever may be thought of Murdoch as an owner of newspapers, he is owed an incalculable debt for breaking the blackmailing hold of the unions on the business, which was ruining newspapers.

An interesting point about the different reading public of The Observer and the News of the World was that both took a serious and intelligent interest in racing and breeding; though the letters from one might come on the headed writing paper of an eminent London club and the other be written on a cheap lined pad – one was on stationery provided by HM Prisons – there was little difference in the quality of thought expressed in them. It is a mistake for journalists to write down to their readers, whoever they are. If they are interested in the subject and do not understand a technical expression or point, they will either find out the meaning from someone else, or write to the author about it. Sub-editors who have no technical knowledge of the matter before them can be a menace if, instead of checking with the writer anything they do not understand, they change it to what they think it should read, producing nonsense. Likewise, when stories appear outside their normal place in the paper, because they are of general interest, and are handed over to a news reporter ignorant of the technical aspect of the subject they should be checked by the usual correspondent in the subject, to ensure that they are not open to ridicule among readers who understand the topic, which often happens. In my racing articles, I concentrated on horses and races, rather than news stories. In fact, the arrangement with *The Observer* was that they would get news items and quotes from the PA and leave me to get on with the rest. This worked well, especially on important days when, owing to our early deadline and telephonic difficulties, it was impossible to glean news and quotes and get in the copy in time as well.

On one occasion, however, I was able to furnish *The Observer* with something of a scoop. I had gone to Deauville to ride in the first running of what is now one of the foremost amateur riders' flat races in France, the Prix Georges Courtois, an event which emanated from a suggestion made by me to Marcel Boussac's racing manager, Francois de Brignac. On arriving I found the place in a turmoil and overflowing with journalists from all over the world. The cause was the presence among the riders of Group Captain Townsend, whose current friendship with Princess Margaret had given rise to a furore of interest among the international Press. After the race, in which I was unplaced, I suddenly realised that here was a story which would probably interest *The Observer*. Dashing back to my hotel I managed to get a call through to the newsroom and dictate a piece, which was published. Townsend seemed a pleasant, unassuming young man. He was a passable amateur rider and appeared to be enjoying the public attention given him: had he not done so he could have avoided it by not taking part.

One of the literary jobs to give me most pleasure was being general manager of *The British Racehorse* from its start in 1949 till it was sold, the last issue appearing in 1980. During the war the late E.E. Coussel of the British Bloodstock Agency invited me to lunch at his home near Lewes to meet Roger de Wesselow, owner of a printing business and *Raceform*. The idea was to discuss the possibility of starting a high-grade magazine on racing and breeding, when circumstances allowed. We agreed that there was room for such a publication, but owing to the difficulties of wartime that was as far as the matter went. In 1948 Roger de Wesselow telephoned me, out of the blue, to say that he and Tom Blackwell, a racing friend from the time that I was at Clarehaven and he at Cambridge, had decided to launch the racing and breeding magazine of which we had spoken at the lunch with Coussel during the war, and asked if I would be interested in being involved in it. I was thrilled at the idea and it was agreed that I should be the general manager. The project came under Turf Newspapers, the firm which flourishes today under Roger de Wesselow's son Ian, and at that time was at 55 Curzon Street, Roger being Chairman and Tom a director. They had bookstalls on most race-courses and a racing bookshop – now in Clarges Street – at the Curzon Street office. The first editor was the late David Livingstone-Learmonth, a knowledgeable, experienced writer on racing, who knew the practical side of the sport from having ridden as an amateur, was well read and had an understanding of art. Before the war he wrote the racing article in the *Illustrated Sporting and Dramatic News* and afterwards covered racing for *Horse and Hound*. He was a generation older than me, having served in the last year of the 1914–18 war, was active, hard-working and dedicated to the task. The magazine was an immediate success. It was well supported by advertisements for yearlings sales and studs, also general advertisers and readers interested in breeding and racing. Our principle was to produce it to as high a quality as possible, with a coloured front cover and, if affordable, colour inside. At one moment before the first issue appeared, Roger de Wesselow got cold feet about the expense of colour on the front cover; and the first mock-up took the form of a black and white reproduction of a photograph of Hyperion, with a blue border. The problem was solved by Jean who, when I showed her the proof of the proposed cover, exclaimed: "You can't possibly have that, it looks just like the cover of the *Nursery World*," a publication which we took for the benefit of our boys' nanny. When this observation was relayed to him, Roger gave way and the first issue appeared with a coloured front cover. Later on, we included colour in the articles. Only flat racing was covered, except for one issue later on, which had a section on N.H. racing. This produced several complaints from readers, especially those abroad, which goes to show how divided the two branches of the sport are.

David Livingstone-Learmonth and I usually wrote an article for each issue, he also dealt with the season's racing; the exception was the Spring Issue, which concentrated on the leading winners of the previous season, depicted in posed photographs and extended pedigrees. While David was responsible for the editorial side, I coped with the advertising. The contents of each issue were agreed between us. In dealing with advertisers I found that politeness, tact and guile produced the best

140

results: we had virtually no bad debts. One lapse by David caused some embarrassment. I had written an article on the Lady Josephine family, for which David chose the pictures and wrote the captions. Our most important advertiser was the whisky firm of Dewar, whose chairman, the late J.A. Dewar, owned one of the most famous members of the Lady Josephine family, Tudor Minstrel, the latter's picture appearing in my article. Unfortunately David absentmindedly captioned Tudor Minstrel as being owned by The Honble Lady Macdonald-Buchanan. Dewar was not best pleased, which was only to be expected, particularly as Buchanan's was a rival whisky firm. However, I managed to placate him and we did not lose his firm's advertisement. David Livingstone-Learmonth died in 1959, being succeeded by Bernard O'Sullivan, Tom Tickler and Michael Seth-Smith, in succession.

The magazine continued to show a good profit throughout the period of which I write, but later with the rising costs of production and the loss of advertising with the appearance of *Stud and Stable* and *Pacemaker*, since breeders shared out their advertising between the three, and those with a financial interest in *Pacemaker* naturally confined their support to the latter, the profit turned to loss. As a result it was sold to a consortium and the name changed to *The European Racehorse*, under which it was published until being closed down in 1990.

It had often occurred to me that there was no standard work on steeplechase riding, to which anyone coming into the game could refer. The beginner had to rely on tips from experienced riders, if he could get them, which is not easy for those from a non-racing background, and upon the hard school of trial and error, the latter sometimes proving unfruitful, if not fatal. There seemed to be room for a text book on the subject, simply propounded and suitably illustrated. I discussed the project with a friend, the sculptor and artist John Skeaping, whom I had met towards the end of the war when he was an Intelligence Officer with the SAS, and who was keenly interested in racing. Apart from using the sport as a subject for his talent, he had ridden in several steeplechases himself and understood the game. The idea appealed to him and we decided to produce a book jointly, he contributing the illustrations, I the text. Hutchinsons agreed to publish it under the title 'Steeplechasing' and it appeared in 1951. I was lucky enough to be able to get valuable, professional opinion and advice, and had the MS read by people who knew the jumping business thoroughly. As a result, the book went well and has since twice been revised and reissued, by J.A. Allen of London, to meet changed times. Over the years it has given me much satisfaction through readers telling me that they have been helped by it. 'Steeple-chasing' was followed by a similar book on flat-race riding, 'From Start to Finish', which also has been reprinted by Allen.

John Skeaping had great ability; he was a contemporary of Henry Moore, who said of him that he was the most naturally talented sculptor he knew, but as opposed to Moore, whose life was devoted entirely to his work, Skeaping, as he writes in his autobiography 'Drawn from Life' had too many interests outside his true calling of sculpture, and was a compulsive gambler.

A sparse, well proportioned, smallish, active man, with good, if weather beaten features, John Skeaping might have been taken for an ex-steeplechase jockey. Apart from his outstanding skill as a sculptor he was a fine draughtsman, an able musician and could turn his hand effectively to almost anything. This diversity of ability and interests prevented him attaining his optimum as a sculptor.

Excellent company, Skeaping spoke several languages, was a good conversationalist and raconteur, if accuracy was sometimes sacrificed for the sake of a good story. Though elected to the Royal Academy he did not receive the approval of the Art Establishment, perhaps because his penchant for animal and racing subjects in his work.

The late Quinny Gilbey did me a good turn by getting me the job of writing the breeding article for the *Sporting Chronicle* after the death of J.B. Robertson, a celebrated writer on the subject who had held the position for many years. I enjoyed the work, since breeding in theory as well as in practice had always interested me, and it led to my getting some commissions in advising breeders and buyers.

When the *Sporting Chronicle* merged with one of the Kemsleys' other papers, I became redundant, but was lucky enough to be taken on in the same capacity by *The Sporting Life*, till I retired.

13

ASPECTS OF BREEDING

Through my connection with breeding I met and made friends whom otherwise I would not have got to know. Chief of these was Jim Joel, one of the most successful owner-breeders of the post-war years, till he dispersed his stud because failing eyesight made it impossible for him to read and study his matings, maintaining his interest in racing through his jumpers. His father, Jack, and his uncle Solly, had been eminent owner-breeders and great rivals during the years between the two wars; but towards the end of his life Jack Joel had let his stud run down by using indifferent sires and breeding from bad mares, and when Jim took over it was on the floor. By getting rid of the bad mares, using the best stallions, rebuilding the great line of Absurdity, through Amuse, and introducing new, well-chosen representatives of successful families, added to good stud management, Jim reversed the downward trend. He had definite ideas: no close inbreeding, great respect for the male line of Polymelus, strict regard for correct conformation, soundness and temperament, well farmed paddocks and careful feeding. He kept to the traditional practice at his Childwickbury Stud near St. Albans of wintering stock in bullock-yards, thus resting the paddocks. All this paid off and he consistently bred a fine type of thoroughbred and won every Classic bar The Oaks, which he lost by the shortest of short heads, when his filly West Side Story was beaten by the French filly Monade, whose owner during the wait for the verdict announced that he would be happy to settle for a dead-heat, but the camera ruled otherwise. Jim always planned his own matings, but liked to discuss them with me, and sometimes asked me for suggestions or advice on buying a mare or filly. This usually occurred staying with him for the races or December Sales at

143

his house, Sefton Lodge, which later he sold to the late Charles St. George; or staying with him for Doncaster or York, where he would take part of Ye Olde Bell Inn at Barnby Moor, at the Spa Hotel at Ripon, or the Majestic at Harrogate, other members of the party being racing friends, such as the late Lord Rosebery, Bunty Scrope, (Lieut. Col. Adrian Scrope, formerly stud manager to Sir Richard Sykes and Lord Derby), and Gerry Feilden (General Sir Randle Feilden, the leading Turf administrator in the Jockey Club of his day), whose sister married my cousin John Galbraith. All have now passed on. To me it was fascinating to hear the talk of old times on the Turf, of famous men and horses of the past with which Jim and Harry Rosebery were familiar; and of the later period experienced by Bunty Scrope, who was racing a few years before I came into the game and was a friend of pre-war days. A neat, small man, always immaculately turned out, with a red carnation in his buttonhole whenever he went racing, Jim Joel ran his houses with smooth efficiency and close attention to detail. He was the perfect host, providing superb food and drink and ensuring the comfort of his guests. It occurred to me that he must have been Mess President to his regiment in the 1914–18 war, which later I discovered to be the case. He kept his staff up to the mark, but they were devoted to him. Unassuming, he did many generous actions of which people were not aware.

Among others brave enough to seek my advice on breeding was the late Walter Burmann, who had a thorough knowledge of the science in general, having for a number of years had a successful herd of cattle, but came into the breeding of horses fairly late in life. He was equally successful in this sphere, his most notable victory being in the Prix de l'Arc de Triomphe with Bon Mot III. The manner in which the mating that produced Bon Mot III came about is interesting. Jim Joel asked me to try to find him a nomination to Ballymoss for his mare Crystal Palace, saying that he could offer a service to Worden II in exchange. I knew that Walter Burmann had a share in Ballymoss, so passed on Jim Joel's offer, which was accepted. The nomination to Ballymoss produced Royal Palace, the best horse in England of his day, and the mating of Walter Burmann's mare Djebel Idra with Worden II resulted in Bon Mot III, the outstanding horse in France of the same era. Both proved rather disappointing at stud, though Royal Palace sired the Queen's Oaks and St. Leger winner Dunfermline, and Bon Mot III got Lassalle who won the Ascot Gold Cup and Prix du Cadran. However, Royal Palace's and Bon Mot III's names crop up in the pedigree of successful horses every now and then.

In a previous chapter is an account of my riding a winner for Stanley Wootton, whom I knew from pre-war days. One of the most knowledgeable men in racing of my time and a first-class trainer, Stanley was an Australian by birth and with his brother Frank, a brilliant jockey who died comparatively young, was brought to England as a boy by his father, Dick, who settled and trained at Epsom. Stanley inherited the property and stable, but also had considerable interests in Australia, among them breeding racehorses.

One day Stanley asked me if I knew of a young mare likely to suit the champion Australian sire Star Kingdom who, running in England as Star King, had been one of the fastest two-year-olds of his day and was by Stardust (by Hyperion). At that time, as mentioned earlier, Pat Dennis and I owned a young mare called Oceana, by Colombo out of Orama (by Diophon). Oceana had won as a two-year-old and was narrowly beaten at three; her form was quite good but some way from the top. She had been covered by Persian Gulf but was barren, so could be covered again to Australian time. Her sire Colombo was a brilliant racehorse who won The Two Thousand Guineas and ran third in The Derby, for which he started a hot favourite; his defeat by Windsor Lad, who won, and Easton caused much controversy since Colombo was shut in at a crucial part of the race and many thought he should have won, blaming his failure on the tactics of his jockey, the Australian Rae Johnstone. My reading of the race was that Windsor Lad won with something in hand and was the better stayer of the two. Colombo was not a particularly successful sire, being in the same category as his own sire Manna, winner of The Two Thousand Guineas and The Derby. However, he was well made, had a pretty good pedigree and, being unfashionable at the time, stood at a modest fee. About the best horse sired by him was British Empire, a good two-year-old who achieved great success as a stallion in South America. Oceana's dam Orama bred 13 winners, her best offspring being Beausite (by Bold Archer), second in The One Thousand Guineas and fourth in The Oaks. Her descendants improved the status of the family and included Nearula and Waterloo, winners respectively of The Two Thousand Guineas and One Thousand Guineas, both out of daughters of Orama.

Oceana was beautifully made, not big but lengthy enough for a brood mare – short-coupled mares seldom do well at stud – full of quality, at the same time strong and robust. Had she not been so correct and attractive I would not have dreamt of putting her up to Stanley, who was a stickler for conformation and never bought a bad individual. He came to see her, examined her meticulously, taking in every detail and making no comment. When he had finished he turned to me, saying "I'll have her." So far as I remember the price we agreed was £1,500, which was a fair one. Oceana's history is typical of the romance and unpredictability of the Turf. She was shipped to Australia, where she failed to get in foal in two successive seasons to Kerry Piper (by Trigo), winner of the Cesarewitch and November Handicap. As a result she was sent up for sale, where she caught a cold and returned unwanted. From then on her fortune soared: mated to Star Kingdom she produced Todman, one of the outstanding racehorses and successful sires of winners and brood mares in modern Australian racing. Oceana also bred Noholme, Shifnal and Faringdon, all good sires and racehorses, Noholme being exported to the USA where, after a distinguished racing career in Australia, he became a leading sire.

Unfortunately I did not keep a representative of the family to continue the female line; the fillies we retained and raced were all moderate, so were sold, but most of them became good brood mares. At that time Pat Dennis and I were breeding for sale and had several mares. Later, when Jean and I had our own stud, she wisely persuaded me to change the policy to breeding to race, pointing out that if we ever bred a really good horse and sold it as a yearling we would get little benefit, because of taxation. As a result we cut down the number of mares, put everything in training unless we thought a yearling was not up to standard, and eventually bred Brigadier Gerard. Had I followed this policy from the beginning, keeping only the Orama family and the Brazen Molly family, I would have done much better in the long run, as Stokes, a good winner and second in The Two Thousand, would have made us a great deal of money by the standards of the times, as well as giving us much enjoyment.

Whatever the policy, a breeder has to cull periodically, to avoid overstocking and overspending; and, owing to the unpredictability of nature, sooner or later he will sell a pearl by mistake. This is one of the hazards of the game and must be faced, so that it is no use complaining when it happens. At least, success in other hands boosts the prestige of the breeder's stud and stock. The owner-breeder has certain advantages over the commercial breeder: he can please himself, paying no attention to fashion; does not have to fatten up his yearlings for sale, which is detrimental to their future racing; can bring them up to be tough by running them out night and day; and can breed stayers if he wishes to do so, a policy that is the kiss of death to breeders for sale. For these reasons owner-bred stock tends to do better than commercially-bred stock in the long run: what ambitious commercial breeder would have used Queen's Hussar, who stood at £250 and sired Brigadier Gerard, undoubtedly one of the best English-bred horse of the century, and The One Thousand Guineas and Prix de Diane winner Highclere? Luck is a dominant factor in breeding – the Duke of Beaufort of the day, an eminent owner-breeder, in answer to William Allison's query as to his opinion on achieving success in breeding, ascribed the whole business to pure luck. While this may be an overstatement, there is more than a little truth in it, as the following story, told me by Bunty Scrope, illustrates. In the 1920s, when Bunty was assistant stud manager at Sledmere, King George V's son-in-law, Lord Harewood, was asked by the King to find two top-class yearling fillies which, at the end of their racing careers, would be likely to make brood mares for the Royal Stud. Harewood asked the stud manager if Sledmere had two such fillies for sale and was told that, in fact, they had a couple which fitted the requirements. He came to see them and, on inspection, termed one "a cart horse", the other "a weed", and departed. The two fillies turned out to be Straitlace, winner of The Oaks, and Mumtaz Mahal, probably the fastest filly of the century, both founding great families, whose descendants are winning top races to this day.

14

SOME PEOPLE

The late Lord Rosebery was one of the most eminent figures in racing of my time. I first knew him when I worked with Victor Gilpin and we had moved from Clarehaven at Newmarket to Michel Grove near Arundel, and Harry Rosebery used to stay at Arundel Castle with Bernard and Lavinia Norfolk, for whom we trained. They all, at some time or other, came over to our stable to ride out and to watch the work. After the war, Jean and I used to go to stay at Mentmore every year to see the yearlings, and we also stayed with the Roseberys at Cleveland House, Newmarket. Well-educated in a generation when erudition was unfashionable in society, Harry Rosebery was extremely able, and the survival of racing during the war owes much to his experience in dealing with Government Ministers and authority, and to his strong character and determination. He knew racing inside out, was not one with whom any liberties could be taken, resented criticism of his horses and could be vindictive. He was successful as an owner-breeder, winning The Derby with his home-bred colts Blue Peter (Fairway-Fancy Free, by Stefan the Great) and Ocean Swell (Blue Peter-Jiffy by Hurry On). He set great store by stamina and toughness, though not averse to using fast milers as sires. Apart from his mental ability, Rosebery was a fine athlete in his youth, good at all games – he captained Surrey at cricket – and was one of the best men to hounds of his day when Master of the Whaddon Chase. But life had not always been easy. His brother Neil, who was killed by a stray shot in the 1914–18 war, was the favourite of his father, the Prime Minister, who never recovered from Neil's death. Added to this, Harry Rosebery had been involved in a racing scandal in 1905, which became known as the Pitch Battle case. On Friday, 27th October

148

1905, a match at Sandown Park took place between Mr. W.F. de Wend-Fenton's Pitch Battle, 5 years, 11st. 4lbs, and Lord Gerard's Piari, 4 years, 10st. 8lbs, over one-and-a-quarter miles, owners up. The form indicated that Pitch Battle had the best chance, but to general surprise Pitch Battle drifted in the betting to such an extent that Piari started favourite at 100–12 on and won by a length. The Racing Calendar's account of the enquiry that followed reads: "After the decision of this Match, the Stewards called on Mr de Wend-Fenton to account for his riding of Pitch Battle. They were not satisfied with his explanation, and decided to refer the case to the Stewards of the Jockey Club for further investigation, and added that, pending further investigation by the Stewards of the Jockey Club, he would not be allowed to ride at Sandown Park, and no horse belonging to him, or in which he had an interest, or was concerned in the management of, would be allowed to run at Sandown. The Stewards of the Jockey Club made further enquiry into the matter, and warned Mr. W.F. de Wend-Fenton off Newmarket Heath – the sentence was extended by the Stewards of the National Hunt Committee to all Meetings under their Rules." An odd aspect of this notice is the suspension by the Sandown Stewards before the case had come up at the Jockey Club. After this it emerged that among those who had backed Piari, and therefore were presumed to have been party to Pitch Battle being stopped, was Harry Rosebery, who thus incurred the anger of his father, who never forgave him. So much so that, as the late Fred Cripps, a friend and contemporary of Harry Rosebery, once told me, when walking with Harry Rosebery and his father, the latter referring to Neil's death, turned to Harry and said, "I wish it had been you."

One evening at Cleveland House I was sitting in the garden with Harry Rosebery after dinner, the other members being in the house playing bridge. It was a beautiful still night and, emboldened by a generous intake of my host's champagne, I said to him: "Tell me, Lord Rosebery, what was the true story of the Pitch Battle case?" He replied: "It was this. Several people had come to my father and asked if he could do anything for this young man de Wend-Fenton, who that year had won The Two Thousand Guineas with Vedas, as he was foolish but not really a rogue; and as a result of my father speaking to the Stewards of the Jockey Club on de Wend-Fenton's behalf, people thought that I was involved." The impression given was that, however true or untrue his account was, we had come to believe it to be correct. I once asked the late Stanley Harrison, a good amateur rider in his youth who was racing about that time, what he made of the Pitch Battle case. "It's quite simple" he said. "The man was too conceited; he pulled the horse up under the judges' nose, instead of putting him to sleep on the far side of the course – like you or I would have done!"

Another social burden upon Lord Rosebery was the opprobrium he aroused among some of his own generation because, in the 1914–18 war, in spite of having won the DSO and MC and being wounded in France, after recovering he accepted an appointment on Allenby's staff in the Middle East, instead of returning to his regiment in the trenches. Only one of exceptional mental toughness and strength of character could have overcome all this, to lead such a vigorous, purposeful life.

15

MORE PEOPLE

A particular attraction of the Turf is the diversity of those drawn into it. Among the owners for whom I have ridden, besides those already mentioned, were: one acquitted of murder; three who did time – one for perjury, another for involvement with a ringer, the third for fraud; three Maharajahs; an eminent Pakistani statesman; a butcher; several Peers of the Realm; a wine merchant; two bookmakers; a rich American alcoholic living in France; a daughter of Rudyard Kipling; a South African gambler; several farmers; members of the Jockey Club; a Chinese restaurateur; a world-famous footballer; two soldiers who became eminent Generals, my wife and myself. Some of these I have written about earlier, others I never met. The man tried for murder was Sir Delves Broughton the chief character in *White Mischief*, accused of murdering Lord Errol and acquitted. He was not present when I rode for him – the horse was placed, but I can't remember its name. Broughton was an effete, weak, fickle man, whom old Porchey Carnarvon, who knew him well, avowed incapable of the ability or resolution to commit murder. The fraudster who was gaoled was a young man called John Hallet, a pleasant-mannered, seemingly harmless if unexciting man, who during the war, as I remember it, sold the trading rights in Burma, on a forged document purporting to have been signed by Mountbatten, to the son of a Maharajah. The stroke was discovered through the security police seeing a junior officer playing in lakhs at a gambling joint in Calcutta, and becoming suspicious. The footballer was Stanley Mathews (now Sir Stanley Mathews), whose horse, Bas Bleu, given him by a fan, won with me at Worcester. The owner was present on the day and I found him a most agreeable, courteous man, whose quiet manner gave no hint of his fame and pre-

151

eminence in his profession. As a memento of his victory he kindly sent me an attractive tea-set from his own pottery. All this added to the entertainment of my riding life. It has long been the case to blame all racing villainy on bookmakers, but it must be realised that it takes two or more to organise any type of fraud; that where there is money there will always be chicanery and that a Tote monopoly would be no guarantee to probity; even in the State-controlled, bookmakerless racing of the Soviet Union fixed races were not unknown. Regarding individual bookmakers, I have written of Horace Lester and Percy Thompson, but the greatest bookmaker of my time was William Hill. From a tough background he had come up the hard way and, I suspect, could be pretty ruthless, but became a respected and distinguished figure on the Turf, not merely as a bookmaker, but as an owner and breeder. The turning point of his career was when he took the view that the odds-on favourite, Big Game, would not stay the distance of The Derby, and laid him beyond hope of settling had the horse won. He was proved correct; after being in the lead at a mile-and-a-quarter, Big Game weakened to finish fourth, the winner being Watling Street. From then on William Hill never looked back. A hard worker and meticulously thorough in everything he took on, he had a flair for book-making, and the courage to back his opinion and lay substantial bets, re-gardless of the price. I was standing near the rails one day at Newmarket, when the late Tommy Carey came up to him and said, "What's mine, Bill?'

"Six to one."

'I'll have six thousand to one."

"Right. Six thousand to one (naming the horse) for T. Carey."

"Seven to one," Hill immediately called out, knocking the horse out a point, somewhat to Carey's consternation and embarrassment. The horse lost. William Hill went into the bloodstock business with charac-teristic vigour and thoroughness. He bought the Whitsbury Manor stud and racing stable, collected a carefully chosen band of mares and used the best stallions. The colts were sold as yearlings and selected fillies retained, raced and returned to stud. His yearling were good indi-viduals, well produced and made good prices; among them were the Two Thousand and Derby winner Nimbus, also Grey Sovereign, one of the best sprinters of his day and a highly successful and influential sire. William also imported the stallions Chanteur II, who got the Derby winner Pinza, also imported by him were Souverain and Gyr. All were good racehorses, bred in France, but the last-named two achieved little at stud. Of his home-bred fillies, the best was the St. Leger winner Cantelo, a daughter of Chanteur II and unfortunate enough to be born the same year as the exceptional Petite Etoile, to whom she ran second in The Oaks. Apart from knowing William Hill on the racecourse, he was an advertiser in *The British Racehorse*, both for his business and his stud. The arrangement came about through my taking him to lunch at the old Mirabelle restaurant in Curzon Street, finding him a most interesting conversationist and a pleasant and business-like man in his dealings. While appreciating good food he ate and drank sparingly.

Tommy Carey, referred to above, was an opportunist and heavy better, who rose from being a stable lad to training. Regrettably, after a long, successful run as a backer, his luck ran out and he ended by committing suicide. Carey started as a lad in Walter Nightingall's stable at Epsom, and when taking a horse to a meeting sometimes gave another lad a few shillings to lead it round while he went into the ring to bet. He advanced to riding at Northolt Park pony races, then was given a licence under the Rules of Racing, winning The Derby for his old master on Miss Dorothy Paget's Straight Deal during the war. Turning to training he survived, still betting heavily till, as related, his fortunes failed and he took his own life. I once rode for him, on a horse called Own Time at Lewes. Noticing that Own Time was entered in a race for amateurs, I telephoned him to ask if it was running and if I could ride it. He replied: "D'you think it'll win?"

"It's got quite a good chance."

"All right, you can ride it."

It did win, but only just, beating a horse ridden by Dick Smalley, then a serving officer in the Royal Marines and later Jockey Club starter, famous as the first owner of the great little 'chaser Halloween, whom Bill Wightman trained to win the King George VI 'Chase twice and be four times placed in the Cheltenham Gold Cup. Own Time was one of the hardest rides I ever had: he hung first one way, then the other, all up the straight, matters not being helped by the ground sloping towards the far rails. I was relieved to see his number go up, as was Tommy Carey who, encouraged by my asking for the ride, had a good bet. One of the reasons why Tommy Carey lasted so long as he did was that he avoided having big bets on short-priced horses and was not afraid to plunge on outsiders if he thought that they had a winning chance. In fact, he had £200 on the last winner I rode over hurdles, Hastener, at Sandown, who started at 20–1. When he told me and I asked however he came to back it, he said: "Well, I saw you lining up on the inside and keen to get a good start, and reckoned that at your age you wouldn't be riding just to go round, so I took a chance."

A colourful personality among the bookmakers of that time was 'Snouty' Parker, a Jewish cockney who looked rather like a less refined edition of the comedian Bud Flanagan. Snouty reached the big time through doing the commission for Blue Peter in The Derby. He was a cheery, amusing, generous individual, though shrewd in business, with a Max Miller sense of humour. One day, between races, he was bending over his ledger with his penciller when a less affluent regular of Tattersalls' ring sidled up to him and said: "I'm not going too good, Snouty, could you let me have some readies to help me along?" Without turning round, looking up to discover the identity of the enquirer, pausing for thought, drawing breath or varying the tone of his voice, Snouty replied: "Readies? I've got readies in every pocket and wives in every port and when I can't fuck no more I'm going to lay down and die how much d'you want?" I first met Snouty flying back from a race meeting, I think it was Chepstow. It was a bumpy flight and his penciller was feeling air-sick and looked it – he had my full sympathy since at that time I suffered the same trouble. However, he got little comfort from his employer who bade him "Get on with them figures and you'll soon forget about feeling sick."

Though a small better, I knew most of the rails bookmakers and never had any altercation over a bet with any of them. I usually bet with Charlie Hunter-Simmons of Heathorns and have carried on the tradition with the present representative of the family, Michael, a successful owner and breeder as well.

Of the racing officials of my time, the one who stands out in my memory is Geoffrey Freer. A tall, well-built figure, then white-haired and with features which would have graced a Roman senator or a bishop, he knew racing through and through, finishing up as Senior Jockey Club Handicapper. Despite his dignified appearance, he was full of wit and humour and was excellent company. As a young man, so 'Gugs' Weatherby told me, Geoffrey had been a live wire, by no means averse to the bright lights, and knowing what it was to get into financial trouble and betting difficulties. All this was in the distant past, and had my informant not been so reliable, I would not have believed it. As Clerk of the Course at Newbury, he used to stay at the Chequers Hotel and often dined with us. He enjoyed a game of bridge, which Jean always arranged for his visits to us. Once when dining at the Chequers at the same table as Frank Byrne, the *Times* racing correspondent, the latter asked him if he was going racing the following day. Geoffrey replied: "I'm going to a point-to-point – naming the meeting – where I think my daughter is riding a good thing in the Ladies Race." At this Frank Byrne, a serious punter, pricked up his ears, reckoning that if the Senior Jockey Club handicapper considered a horse a certainty for a point-to-point, it really must be something to bet on. So he drew a substantial amount of ready money from the bank, went to the point-to-point the following day and put it on the said horse. It was beaten a short head – by Limber Hill, winner the following year of the Cheltenham Gold Cup.

A character from a past age and one of the most eminent figures on the Turf of my time was the late Lord Sefton. Tall, handsome, aristocratic, arrogant, a former Field Master of the Quorn, a keen owner under both Rules, an excellent and conscientious Steward, the leading figure in the coursing world and winner of a Waterloo Cup, he was always immaculately turned out, even to the highly-polished case holding his race glasses. He had, I believe, a certain chip on his shoulder because he went to Harrow, when most of his friends and associates were old Etonians. Scrupulously loyal to his trainers and jockeys – he refused to put me up on a hurdler in place of his usual jockey, whose style of riding Harry Brown, the horse's trainer, thought would not suit the horse so well as mine: the horse won – Lord Sefton made a point of going to see his runners, however indifferent, whenever possible. Fond of his horses, he continued to breed them on his property near Liverpool, despite the adverse environment, because he enjoyed having the young stock around him. He never asked a stallion owner for a nomination, only using horses whose services were offered him personally. As a result, his success as a breeder was limited. Accustomed, when training with Atty Persse, to never having to pay a training bill, as a result of his winnings from the stable's betting commissions, he was somewhat taken aback to find this system no longer worked when he had to change trainers after Persse's death. An instance of his arrogance was related to me by Dick Scrope, who knew Sefton well and used to shoot with him every year. One such year Dick had a letter inviting him to shoot on a certain date. He accepted and arrived on the day stated, only to find no-one there except the Keeper, who informed him that the shoot was on the following day. When Sefton chided Dick for being so stupid as to turn up on the wrong day, he produced the letter, which quoted the day on which he arrived. "He never spoke to me for a year," Dick told me. Yet Sefton had a keen, dry wit, as the many stories told of him show. Most of these are familiar, but one may not be so well known.

At a Jockey Club meeting, candidates for membership were being considered, their suitability being outlined by their proposers – a system no longer in use. One of the candidates was the late Peter Fitzwilliam (then Lord Milton), who a few years earlier had been up before the Stewards over the running of one of his horses. His proposer, Lord Zetland, was explaining that though his nephew had been in trouble in the past he was sure that, if elected, he would realise his responsibilities fully and prove a useful member of the Club, when from Lord Sefton came the observation: "the first time I've heard of the Club being used as a Borstal institution." Despite all this, he was not without compassion, as Jean discovered when, pregnant, looking worried and unhappy when standing in the parade ring as I went out on Cloncarrig for the 'National, Lord Sefton put his arm round her shoulders and said, "Don't worry, my dear, it won't be long and he'll be quite all right."

Shortly before these words were written, there died a friend from my wartime days in Phantom, Professor Michael Oakeshott, who was a keen follower of racing, the most distinguished philosopher of his day, head of the London School of Economics and a most entertaining and unusual character. Small, neat, unassuming, witty and merry, few in Phantom were aware of his academic distinction, among them Peregrine (now Sir Peregrine) Worsthorne who, having held forth on politics in general to a group of brother officers, including Oakeshott, was somewhat taken aback, when attending a lecture of importance on a similar subject after the war, to find the speaker was Michael Oakeshott. As head of the LSE, it was unusual to find him a Conservative, for which party Michael voted on the principle that "it did least damage." He and a friend, Guy Griffith, another academic, disconcerted more than a few headmasters who issued the work of Oakeshott and Griffith, *A Guide to the Classics*, to their VI forms, only to find it was a treatise on how to back the winner of The Derby. His practical wit and ingenuity were made evident on the occasion of an address by a new C.O. of Phantom, who was going on interminably, boring everyone present, who longed for escape. Suddenly Michael Oakeshott scribbled something on a scrap of paper and had it passed up to the speaker. On the paper was written BUFFS, which was an unofficial code among Phantom WT operators signifying a demand to speed up transmission. Puzzled, the C.O. asked what BUFFS stood for and was informed: "Buck up for fuck's sake." It had the desired result. There was a story that Oakeshott was meant to receive a title, but by mistake it went to another man of the same name. If true, I think that the error would have amused rather than disappointed him.

16

WEIGHED IN FOR THE LAST TIME

1956 saw the finish of my race riding career. Two factors contributed to ending it: difficulty in keeping fit and trouble from my back. Though having no weight problems and being a non-smoker, I found it impossible to reach the necessary physical condition by riding work a couple of mornings a week and in only a dozen or less races a year, which the diminishing number open to amateurs on the flat dictated. Having given up riding over obstacles, the winter offered no scope for practice and, as every jockey knows, the only way to get fit for race riding is riding in races. The trouble from my back traced to the fall of Kami at Lingfield. It did not appear until a day or two after, when emerging from the cinema my back was gripped in a painful spasm and I found it difficult to straighten up. An osteopath put it right, but it continued to bother me periodically, after falls or through other causes, such as lifting objects carelessly and, sometimes, just sneezing. While treatment was a temporary cure, my back began to go out of place more and more easily, until merely sitting down in the saddle was liable to cause it; so that I could not ride out from the yard with safety, but had to get straight on to the horse at the training ground and stand up in the irons still dismounting. Otherwise there was a risk of displacement. By then I was 46, which did not help matters.

In my last season I managed to head the list of amateurs on the flat for the 13th time in succession, two being pre-war and three joint-top – one with Teddy Underdown, another with Frank Cundell, a third with Peter Bennett – but rode only four winners, one more than Gay Kindersley, and reached my 100th winner on the flat in England and my eighth consecutive victory in the Carnarvon Cup. My 100th winner was at

Wolverhampton on Carino, a handsome, powerful, bay colt owned by Miss Grizel Grant-Lawson, a Master of the Pytchley and sister of Sir Peter Grant-Lawson, who was a member of the National Hunt Committee (now merged with the Jockey Club) and a good amateur rider in his day. Carino's win gratified me especially because the stable from which he came was managed by Lavinia (Lavinia Duchess of Norfolk), whom with her husband, Bernard (Duke of Norfolk), who died in 1975, I had known from happy pre-war days with Victor Gilpin at Michel Grove, who trained for the Norfolks on Bernard's property. A sister to Ronnie Belper, Lavinia was a first-class horsewoman, excelling in all branches of equitation, including riding racehorses work.

Though rather solemn in appearance and demeanour, Bernard Norfolk was not without quiet humour: when asked by an interviewer what would happen if it rained on the day of the Queen's coronation he replied: "We would all get very wet."

After the war the Norfolk's stable was moved to Arundel, where it is now run by John Dunlop, who trains for Lavinia.

The Norfolks created a stud at Arundel, which continues and has bred them many winners. The best product of the stud was Castle Keep, winner of the Ascot Gold Cup, a victory particularly treasured by Bernard on account of his association with Ascot as the Queen's Representative there. Also from the stud, called the Angmering Park Stud, came The St. Leger winner Moon Madness and Sheriffs Star (Coronation Cup). After the race the Stewards graciously invited Grizel and myself to have a drink to celebrate the victory. We repaired to the Stewards' luncheon room, where seated was Harry Brown, who as an amateur in the 1920s became the last to head the list of winning N.H. riders including professionals, and for whom I had ridden a winner over fences when he was training before the war. Now retired, he had been made a Patron of Wolverhampton in recognition of his many successes over the course, his local one, as a rider and a trainer. Reclining in an armchair, he was drinking a large glass of port, which the glow of his complexion and his relaxed, benign manner suggested was not his first. Handsome, debonair, still in good physical shape and, as ever, elegantly dressed, he spoke with a drawl reminiscent of the gilded young men of the 1920s and might have stepped out of one of Frederick Lonsdale's plays. His greeting was warm, if in the circumstances somewhat embarrassing, in view of amateurs being forbidden to accept money: "Well done Grizel old girl; in my day we used to think a hundred quid fair and we liked it pretty sharp after the race"; and in an aside to me: "I've done my best for you, old boy." His remarks were discreetly overlooked. However, I later received one of Carino's racing plates beautifully mounted and appropriately inscribed.

Looking back on my riding career, there are many aspects in which my performance could have been improved. It is a fact of life that amateurs quite often have become successful professionals, even champions, under N.H. Rules, but for one to do the same on the flat is unknown. However, I was once paid the unusual compliment of being pronounced *better* than the flat race professionals. It came about in this way: Reg Butchers, formerly secretary to Tom Masson and Towser Gosden, father of the present-day trainer John Gosden, was standing beside a couple of punters at a meeting on the now defunct Lewes racecourse. One asked his friend: "What are you going to back here?" The other replied "I think I'll have a bit on the one Johnny Hislop rides." To this came the rejoinder: "Oo, you want to be careful, he can stop 'em better than any professional!"

Alas, it is improbable that this glittering if backhanded accolade can be attributed to unbiased, informed criticism. Like many of the racing public, the speaker was clearly one of those who believe every beaten favourite to be crooked and every long-priced winner a coup, and was doubtless basing his assessment on having backed a favourite ridden by me, which failed to win. As it was, with the few opportunities for amateurs on the flat, I was only too anxious to ride a winner if I could, when I could and where I could.

On the flat, it was only towards the end of my race riding days, through the advice of the greatest of all tutors of jockeys, Stanley Wootton, that I developed something approaching the classical style of the Wootton school: short stirrup-leathers, but not so that the knees came above the withers; seat close to the saddle; elbows and toes in; wrists up, as in holding a tennis racquet in play; back straight, crouch low as possible consistent with ability to see ahead; contact with the horse's mouth maintained except, possibly, in the last strides of a desperate finish; if looking round, turn only the head, never the body; sit as still as possible during the race; when riding a horse out with hands and heels, keep strictly in rhythm with the horse's stride; use the whip in the correct hand, parallel with the horse's flank – not waved above the head like a tennis racquet during service, or wide out to the side; swing the whip once or twice, to give the horse a chance to run on without being hit; hit the horse in rhythm, every other stride, and behind the stifle, but not excessively: the finest exponent of the use of the whip in my experience was Joe Mercer. I had more or less mastered these principles by the end of my race riding time, but lack of fitness and practice on the racecourse prevented me from reaching anything approaching professional standard.

Over hurdles, when riding regularly under N.H. Rules, some critics rated me as good as the professionals. Over fences I was far too insecure. My experience in riding work and racing on the flat enabled me to become reasonably proficient in a finish, but this avails a jockey nothing if he is on the floor. In any case, I was not strong enough to do justice to big, powerful, hard pulling 'chasers. Tactically, I was fairly sound and could be relied upon to carry out riding instructions, but tended to become unduly impatient waiting for an opening to appear. All this took place during a period of limited scope for amateurs on the flat, being between the time when amateurs could ride against professionals under Jockey Club Rules, provided the authorities approved their competence, and before the present when there are more races open to them at home and many abroad for those able to make use of these opportunities. Still, I have no cause for complaint: I had much enjoyment, only one serious accident, a measure of success, gained valuable experience of many aspects of racing and made numerous friends in different branches of the sport.

My final winner was at Ayr on Tickled Pink, of whom I have written; a few days earlier on September 15th 1956, in the Horse Shoe Plate, one mile and three furlongs, at Worcester – a course now confined to jumping – I won on an attractive, bay 4-year-old colt, Bois Merida (by Bois Roussel-Merida by Jock II), trained by Peter Thrale. Peter told me to ride the horse sympathetically, as he had been punished in some of his previous races, losing confidence as a result. I had never ridden Bois Merida before, but felt in tune with him from the moment of landing in the saddle. He had a great front and a long, easy stride which begged for a good length of rein; ridden thus, he moved smoothly and kindly to the post. Possibly Bois Merida had a reputation for unreliability, since he was easy to back at 3–1, being joint favourite with Friarspark, ridden by Gay Kindersley, and Marly Knowe under Harold Wallington Jnr, who a few years later was drowned swimming in the sea. Bois Merida was sweating at the post, perhaps in anticipation of chastisement during the race, so I sat quietly on him, with a light hold on the reins, gave him a pat and spoke kindly to him, trying to assure him that he was about to receive persuasion and not punishment. Allowed to run the race as he pleased, Bois Merida moved easily into the lead after a furlong, going sweetly and effortlessly. So we continued. Turning into the straight, he took a stronger hold and quickened his pace. Coming into the last furlong, out of the corner of my eye I saw Marly Knowe creeping up on us. For a second, the thought came to give Bois Merida one smack to ensure victory. Wisely I desisted, since it might have cost us the race, the chances being that Bois Merida would have resented it and curled up. As it was, he ran on courageously to win by a head. The form-book read 'cleverly', but I doubt whether he could have pulled out any more: his long stride was not adapted to sudden acceleration, and he was galloping at full stretch. This was the only race Bois Merida won that year.

My last ride was on Carino, who had given me my 100th winner on the flat in England. Peter Thrale's brother Dick, grandfather of the excellent N.H. rider Richard Dunwoody, had asked me to ride Jai Pet, but I felt that I ought to stay with Carino, though he appeared to have trained off. As it turned out, Jai Pet won, ridden by John Bosley, and Carino, who was never going well, finished fourth. The result was in keeping with the end of my race riding days: the guttering out of a brief candle on a dark, damp, dreary, autumn afternoon. It would have been nice to have finished with a winner, but this might have encouraged me to soldier on, which would have been a mistake. At least a decade older than most of my fellow amateurs, I carried the penalties of latening middle age, lack of fitness and race riding practice, and a legacy of past falls. All this held no promise for the future, bringing home the realisation that, as a jockey, to paraphrase Sassoon: "I had seen death; I knew that I had lived too long."

RECORD ON THE FLAT 1946–56

ENGLAND

Year	WON	2nd	3rd	unplaced	total
1946	13	1	–	4	18
1947	12	6	4	6	28
1948	15	6	5	8	34
1949	8	8	2	4	22
1950	9	1	2	2	14
1951	7	1	2	5	15
1952	4	7	1	1	13
1953	3	1	2	4	10
1954	5	1	1	2	9
1955	7	–	1	–	8
1956	4	1	–	1	6
	87	33	20	37	177

ABROAD; NORWAY – 1 winner, 1945; HAMBURG – 1 (4th)
OSTEND – 1 winner; DEAUVILLE – 1 (unplaced); LE TREMBLAY – 1 (2nd);

N.H. RECORD 1945–50

Year	WON	2nd	3rd	unplaced	total
1945	2	2	3	6	13
1946	5	1	2	15	23
1947	2	4	2	9	17
1948	4	5	2	15	26
1949	4	–	2	6	12
1950	1	4	–	4	9
	18	16	11	55	100

INDEX